Fritz Ridenour

How To

What's Really Important

Without giving up the things that are

GL Regal Books

A Division of G/L Publications
Glendale, California, U.S.A.

Other good Regal reading by Fritz Ridenour:
How to Be a Christian in an Unchristian World
How to Be a Christian Without Being Religious
How Do You Handle Life?
The Other Side of Morality
Tell It Like It Is
So, What's the Difference?
I'm a Good Man, But . . .
Who Says?
Faith It or Fake It?

Scripture quotations in this publication, unless otherwise
noted, are from the *New American Standard Bible.* © The
Lockman Foundation 1960, 1962, 1963, 1968, 1971. Used
by permission. Other versions quoted are:
TLB From *The Living Bible*, Copyright © 1971 by Tyndale
House Publishers, Wheaton, Illinois. Used by permission.
Phillips The New Testament in Modern English, Revised
Edition, J.B. Phillips, Translator. © J.B. Phillips 1958,
1960, 1972. Used by permission of Macmillan Publishing Co.,
Inc.
AMP Amplified Bible, The. Copyright © 1962, 1964 by
Zondervan Publishing House. Used by permission.
KJV King James Version

Published by Regal Books Division, G/L Publications
Glendale, California 91209
Printed in U.S.A.

Library of Congress Catalog Card No. 78-68146
ISBN 0-8307-0266-0

TABLE OF CONTENTS

A Teacher's Manual and Student Guide for use with this book are available from your church supplier.

To Amy, Bill, Doug, Jim, Mark,
Michelle, Paul, Randy, Roy, Ruth, Tim
and the hundreds of other high school students
who have helped me learn
how to decide what's really important,
without giving up the things that are.

WHAT'S SO IMPORTANT ABOUT VALUES?

"Compare my values to what Jesus taught? No way! All I'll feel is guilty!"

That was the comment I got from a tall, sandy-haired fellow when I talked with him and some of his friends about writing a book on "Christian values." How, I wanted to know, could a book help people think through their values in a practical, helpful way? Would the teachings of Christ give readers of the book the kind of help they needed or would His words seem too unrelated to life today?

I wasn't amazed by the "no way!" response. It is a little threatening to examine something as personal as your values, especially when using the teachings of Jesus as a mirror. We are afraid He will show up our spiritual "zits" and our moral scars. Almost instinctively we know that our values and His values probably aren't the same.

WHAT ARE VALUES ANYWAY?

"Values are something you hold above other things. Your values cause you to act on your own rather than doing something someone else suggested."

"Something I believe in strongly enough to act on. If I don't act on it, it is not really a value."

"Values come first, then morals. You have your values and then decide how you are going to act."

The preceding comments were made by high school students I talked with about this book. And they all say one thing: values go very deep. Everyone connects values with actions, not just beliefs. It is not a case of reciting the Apostles' Creed or repeating the Ten Commandments and saying "*These* are my values!" You have to *live* your values, not just recite them. For example, try spending some time with another person. Do things together and talk together. Try to compete with one another in some kind of game or sport. Both of you will soon have a much better picture of each other's real values.

WHERE IS THIS BOOK COMING FROM?

The major question this book will try to answer is, "How do we get—and keep—the 'right' values?" We all have different standards, different ideas of what is really important. Who is to say what is "right"?

There is only one possible source to which the Christian can turn to learn the "right values": God, whom we know through Jesus Christ. So, in this book we will let the Bible—especially the teachings of Jesus—be our base of authority and our source for finding principles to live by. Note that I said "principles," not rules or regulations. The worst mistake Christians can make is to try to reduce their values to a list of proof texts and memory verses. There is a big difference between making God's Word your source of authority and forcing it to become a rule book for every situation. The first time you hit something the Bible doesn't refer to specifically (abortion, for example), you're stuck.

I'm also making the assumption that if you're bothering to read this book, you're a Christian, or at least you're interested in what a Christian is and does. In each chapter we will take a look at a problem or question that concerns most Christians. Then we'll see what Jesus had to say about it and how we can apply the principles He taught in the first century to our particular situation in the twentieth.

Don't worry about Jesus' teachings on values turning into a big guilt trip. I respect the feelings of the gun-shy young man quoted earlier, but there is really no point in saying we're Christians and then hiding from our Saviour and Lord. He knows all about our values anyway and He wants to help us change them where it is necessary. But He doesn't force Himself on any of us. He is there to help *if we want Him to*.

WHERE IS THIS BOOK GOING TO TAKE YOU?

In addition to the teaching of Jesus, every chapter

includes two helpful sections. I call one section "So Where Do I Go from Here?" This section includes brief, easy-to-do questionnaires and quizzes that will help you see how much you value certain beliefs, ideas, people and things. What is *really* important to you? You may be surprised by some of your own answers.

The other section in each chapter is called "And What Can I Do About All This?" Here I try to zero in on some practical ideas you can put into action right now, to strengthen some of your values, or start changing others. We don't change our values overnight; they are part of our habits, our life-style. It's never easy to break a bad habit or form a new and positive one. But to paraphrase that old Chinese saying about getting started on a thousand-mile trip, "Journey toward more Christ-centered values begins with small steps." We list some ideas for taking those first small steps, if you want to use them. Better yet, the Holy Spirit may give you your own ideas for improving your life. And those are the best kind of all.

No one book can cover every problem or question, but I do hope to make a start on helping us think about something that is absolutely crucial in everyone's life—values. Reduced to the bare minimum, values are what we feel is important. And what we feel is important is what drives us to do (or not do) certain things.

Values are what caused Bruce Jenner to spend literally thousands of hours in the most exhausting kind of training in order to bring home, in 1977, an Olympic gold medal in the decathlon.

ARE MY VALUES
WHAT THEY
SHOULD BE?

Values are what caused one group of youths to shoot an ice cream vendor when he refused their demands for money. And values are what caused some bystanders to rush to the man's aid, while others, from very young to near-adult, raided the truck and carried off an undetermined amount of ice cream.[1]

Values are what cause a girl to move in with a guy to "live together" without a marriage commitment. Values turn one man into a missionary, another into a hijacker of airliners.

There are all kinds of values that can be a part of anyone's life. And there is a lot of disagreement in this world about which values are the right ones to hold. Every Christian, however, faces a basic question: Are my values what they should be? Am I living according to the teaching of Christ and the Bible? Those aren't easy questions, but the answers are there — if we're not afraid to look.

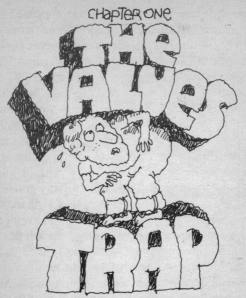

CHAPTER ONE

How Do I Battle the "Big Squeeze"?

"How can I cope in this huge pressure cooker called the world?"

Just about everybody is asking that question, including most of those who call themselves Christians. In fact, life in the world's pressure cooker has special challenge and meaning to every believer. As any follower of Christ knows, being a Christian is not easy. God's grace and salvation are free, but there is a daily price to pay called "trust and obey." Christians are taught to walk a fine line labeled "*in* the world, but not *of* it." We are expected to perform—get good grades, make the team, find a job, earn our keep, pay our bills and taxes. In general, we are supposed to operate successfully in a success-oriented world.

But, at the same time Christians are supposed to stay on center spiritually. Concern about money, popularity, position, status, etc., should never come between us and Christ. We are to guard against letting the world squeeze us into its own mold.[1]

And squeeze us the world does. In fact, "worldliness" is a good candidate for Top Temptation of this or any other year. The trouble is we don't really believe this. We are so busy running the daily rat race we don't always notice how TV and other media are brainwashing us to conform more and more to worldly values and standards. There are so many goodies to enjoy, so many fantastic things to try, that the world's mold slips on quite nicely. We don't even get the sensation of being squeezed. It's a perfect fit.

WHAT DID JESUS SAY ABOUT VALUES?

Television, newspapers and magazines were not around when Jesus walked the dusty roads of Palestine with His disciples. Did He have any concerns about His followers getting squeezed into the worldly mold? Indeed He did and nowhere did He make it clearer than in the Sermon on the Mount.

Conditions were different when Jesus taught His Sermon on the Mount, but people were the same then as they are now. Jesus wanted to warn us against a way of thinking that could easily ruin our relationship with Him. This attitude can take two forms: (1) You can just out and out love the things and experiences this world offers; (2) You can spend a great deal of your time being anxious about having enough of the world's goods to "make it."[2] Either way the devil has your mind *off what God wants* and *on what you want,*

11

WORLDLINESS IS GETTING YOUR MIND OFF WHAT GOD WANTS AND ON ONLY WHAT YOU WANT.

which is precisely what happened to Adam and Eve in the Garden. The result was the Fall. And the whole human race has been a sucker for worldliness ever since. So, it's not at all surprising that Jesus had this to say:

> Do not lay up for yourselves treasures upon earth, where moth and rust destroy, and where thieves break in and steal; but lay up for yourselves treasures in heaven, where neither moth nor rust destroys, and where thieves do not break in or steal; for where your treasure is, there will your heart be also (Matt. 6:19-21).

When Jesus talked about "laying up treasures on earth," He described three basic sources of wealth in Palestine: clothing or fine fabrics; food, especially grain; and money, silver and gold. Jesus reminded His listeners that none of these items could last. Fine fabrics could be destroyed by moths. In verse 19, the Greek word translated "rust" is *brosis*, which means "to eat away." Jesus knew that grain and other goods could be eaten by mice, rats, locusts, grasshoppers, etc. And, of course, thieves could always break in and steal one's possessions. In Palestine at that time "breaking in" wasn't done with jimmies or lock picks. Thieves waited until the homeowner was gone and then literally broke right through the clay walls of the house![3]

What Jesus was saying is that nothing in this world is permanent. It can be destroyed; it can wear out; it can be stolen. Ultimately, He was warning against more than accumulating money and things. Earthly treasures can include people, popularity, status, glory —anything that comes first in our lives. He was talking about a value system turned upside down, where the less important is put ahead of the really important.

We can see this today in our own society where entertainers are paid far larger salaries than are civic leaders, doctors, lawyers, preachers and teachers. One cartoonist summed it up nicely when he showed two old ladies talking. Said one: "Isn't it a shame? They signed a baseball player to a salary higher than the President's!" The other replied: "Why not? He had a better year!"[4]

Sylvester Stallone, writer, producer and star of the box office smash, *Rocky*, found overnight success after living penniless in a rat-infested slum. Did the stardom, the success and the money satisfy? Said Stallone: "Stardom is trash! It's all trash, a load of rubbish!"[5]

What, Then, Are Treasures in Heaven?

No matter how great your fame, wealth or achievements, treasures on earth are never enough to satisfy. On the other hand, says Jesus, you can lay up treasures in heaven, which never wear out, never get eaten or stolen. What does He mean?

The treasure in heaven most Christians think of first is salvation, and certainly Jesus was talking about that. But it is important to remember that laying up treasures in heaven doesn't mean you can get there by doing good works. Christians are saved by grace (God's unlimited favor and mercy). Salvation is a gift of God when we believe in Christ (see Eph. 2:8,9). But (and it's a "but" that is sometimes too easy to forget) Christians are saved to do good works because that is God's plan for every believer (see Eph. 2:10).

So, when Jesus talked about laying up treasures in heaven He was also thinking about living the kind of life God wants us to live. Later in the sixth chapter of Matthew, Jesus described this kind of living as seeking first the Kingdom of God and His righteousness (see Matt. 6:33). How well Christians do this kind of seeking determines their character, their view of life, the inner qualities that make them who they are.

During the Decian persecution of the Christians in A.D. 286 Roman soldiers broke into a Christian church and demanded that Laurentius, the deacon, show them the church's treasures. Laurentius pointed to the hungry being fed, the sick being cared for and said, "These are the treasures of the Church."[6]

Does this mean that we should feed the poor and

help the sick? Yes, whenever possible. Jesus said that those who give a drink of water or something to eat to the least of his brethren do it for Him as well (see Matt. 25:31-46). It could also mean that we should make it a point to reach outside ourselves in many ways to help others in our own families, churches, schools, towns—wherever we have the opportunity. Sometimes the best "cup of cold water" is giving a friendly smile to the new kid in class or doing one of those nitty-gritty chores around home without being asked (or bribed).

There is a rather grim Spanish proverb that contains a lot of truth: "There are no pockets in a shroud." In other words, when you die you carry nothing from this world but *you*. Even your body is left behind. If all your interests have been *here* (on earth) you won't be ready for *there* (heaven).

It's no wonder Jesus points out that where your treasure is, there will your heart be also. No verse in the entire Bible sums up Christian values better than this. Whatever we consider truly important is what captures our time, our energy, our hearts and our minds.

What do we think about most? Where do we spend our time and what do we do with it, especially the leisure hours?

How Clean Are Your Windows?

As Jesus continues He gives another valuable tip on how to resist being squeezed into the world's own mold:

> *The lamp of the body is the eye; if therefore your eye is clear, your whole body will be full*

of light. But if your eye is bad, your whole
body will be full of darkness. If therefore the
light that is in you is darkness, how great is
the darkness! (Matt. 6:22,23).

Jesus is using symbolism and imagery here to teach something very important. He is saying that your eye—how you look at things—is the window of your soul. The cleaner the window, the more light that comes in. If your eye is clear—if you are living in a way that lays up treasures in heaven—you will be full of light. But if your eye is clouded and begrimed by materialism, pride, conceit, selfishness, greed, etc., you will be full of spiritual darkness. "And oh, how *deep* that darkness can be!" (Matt. 6:23, *TLB*).

Serve God or ???

To clinch the whole thing Jesus adds one more thought:

No one can serve two masters; for either he
will hate the one and love the other, or he will
hold to one and despise the other. You cannot
serve God and Mammon (Matt. 6:24).

These are plain words. When it comes to following Christ you have a clear choice. You can serve Him or you can serve Mammon, which is also translated "money" or "material things." You can be His disciple or you can be squeezed into the world's own mold.

When Jesus used the word "Mammon" He knew just what kind of impact it would have on His listeners. There had been a time in the past when mammon had meant "something to be entrusted to someone who would keep it safe." But by the time Jesus walked the earth Mammon was spelled with a capital "M" and had come to mean "that in which I put my trust." In other words, Mammon was no less than a god.[7]

Take a minute to think about the mammon in your own life. What "gods" may be crowding out the real God or leaving Him very little of your time or interests?

SO WHERE DO I GO FROM HERE?

So far we have established a couple of basics:

First, the world's mold is pressing in on Christians harder yet more subtly than ever before.

Second, Jesus knew what the world could do to a Christian and He warned us against it. Where our treasure is, there will our hearts be also. We cannot serve God and Mammon (material things).

So how do we apply Jesus' words to where we are today? Are we to flee the world? Become ascetics or hermits who have nothing to do with anyone? Should we live like a modern-day Simeon Stylites[8], sitting at the top of a pole and never coming down?

And how can we find the "right" values? Is it even possible? One high school group I talked with had comments like these:

AMY: What values should be important in *my* life?

TIM: Different values apply to different people, so it would be impossible to say which values were right and wrong.

JIM: Why should I care if I don't have the so-called right values?

All these comments show that values are hard to

pin down. Still, we are quite certain there is a real difference between earthly (worldly) values and heavenly (spiritual) ones. One way to start discovering and living the "right" values is to see how our own ideas and opinions match up with what Jesus said in Matthew 6:19-24.

For example, on a scale of 1 to 10 how would you rate yourself in regard to the following three questions?

I work hardest at laying up

| 1 | 2 | 3 | 4 | 5 | 6 | 7 | 8 | 9 | 10 |

treasures   treasures
on earth   in heaven

(Go ahead, be honest. And remember, marking the line right in the middle is a cop-out.)

My life-style conforms more closely with

| 1 | 2 | 3 | 4 | 5 | 6 | 7 | 8 | 9 | 10 |

the world   God's will

(Remember, mark where you actually are, not where you would like to be.)

As I move through my usual weekly routine I find myself concerned with

| 1 | 2 | 3 | 4 | 5 | 6 | 7 | 8 | 9 | 10 |

Mammon   serving God
(material things)

(One way to think about this one is to estimate how often you bring God into your daily routine rather than just being swept along with the pressures, the schedules, the deadlines and "getting everything done.")

The major temptation when answering questions like those above is to fudge a little toward the spiritual side. Ask these questions aloud in the typical Sunday School class and almost everyone will give answers that make him look like a "good Christian," or at least no worse than the rest. Keep in mind that as you answer each question in private you can be as honest as you can stand. It's difficult to be totally honest; sometimes we aren't even sure what "totally honest" is. On some days we might answer those three questions one way; on other days the answers would be quite different.

But, to get some value out of all this, try to think of your general pattern, what you usually do, whom you usually associate with, what you usually say to family, friends or strangers.

Now that you've gotten the hang of it, try taking three more looks at your values:

To me, money is

1	2	3	4	5	6	7	8	9	10

not very   supremely
important   important
(Nothing is trickier than money. We all want it; we all need it. The real question is: "Do I control my money, or does it control me?")

As a rule I use my time

1	2	3	4	5	6	7	8	9	10

wastefully   wisely
(Careful on this one. Maybe you need to keep track of your time for a few days to see where it really goes. Once wasted, time is gone forever.)

I am using my mental and physical abilities at the rate of

1	2	3	4	5	6	7	8	9	10

very little   full capacity

(Psychologists pretty well agree that we use only a small percentage of our potential abilities. Another way of asking the question is, "Am I doing the best I can?")

AND WHAT CAN I DO ABOUT ALL THIS?

When thinking about your values it's possible to take one of three approaches:

The ho hum approach takes the attitude that "Well, my values are my values. I do pretty well. It's pretty hard to say where I am in regard to this stuff. There's no need to get in a stew."

The overwhelmed breathless approach says: "Good grief! There's just too much here to think about. It's all too much for me. I wouldn't know how to start carving this stuff down to size. I better just stand pat."

The happy medium approach, however, says this: "I'll pick one, maybe two or three things to work on. I know I'm not up to par with Jesus' values. Nobody is, but He loves me anyway. I can work on some things without feeling my whole life is a guilt trip."

So, go over your answers. Where can you start laying up more treasures in heaven, fewer on earth? In what specific way can you break out of the worldly mold and seek more of God's will? How can you start serving Mammon (material things) *less* and God *more*? What about the way you look at money, time and your abilities? How could you use any of these more effectively?

Here are just a few starter ideas for specific steps you might take right now to change some of your values, strengthen others:

1. Pray daily, asking God to reveal to you where your values are weak or even just plain rotten. Ask Him to help you change.

2. Do more Bible reading and study. Any number of plans are available. Ask your pastor or youth director for ideas.

3. Try budgeting your money on the 10-80-10 plan (give 10 percent to the Lord, live on 80 percent, put 10 percent in savings).

4. Try cutting TV watching time by 10 percent each week. For example, if you are watching ten hours of television, cut it to nine and engage in some other constructive activity. After you succeed at cutting 10 percent, try for 20 percent or even more, depending on your viewing habits. Also analyze what you are watching. Try switching channels and find programs that are more worthwhile.

5. Try reaching out to others in a specific way. Is there someone you should write to? Is there someone you should go visit?

Those are just a few ideas; you can think of many more. The important thing is that whatever you choose, it's something that you know you should do.

As my friend Tim put it, different values apply to different people. The important thing is that you are sure you are taking positive steps toward better values. It's impossible to avoid the big squeeze applied by the world because we live in it daily. But we don't have to give in. We don't have to be molded into conformists who go along with wrong values just because everybody else is doing it or because it's just easier to get along that way. Following is a personal paraphrase of Romans 12:2 based on the *Phillips* translation. Memorize it and repeat it as a daily prayer.

Lord, I don't want the world to squeeze me into its mold. Remold my mind from within and prove in practice that your plan for me is good, that it meets all your specifications and that it moves me toward spiritual maturity.

When it comes to values the important thing for the Christian is to concentrate on letting God remold his or her mind from within. If the Christian does that, the worldly mold will have little effect. As God remolds our minds we prove in practice that His plan for us is good and we become mature—complete in Christ.

The choice is ours: the world's mold or God's remolding from within. Values are always something we choose. As Jesus put it:

WHERE YOUR TREASURE IS,
THERE WILL YOUR HEART BE ALSO.

CHAPTER TWO

FIRST THINGS FIRST

How Do I Straighten Out My Priorities?

When talking about values you almost have to talk about priorities in the same breath. According to Webster, priorities are "an order of preference based on urgency, importance or merit." In other words, your priorities are things you choose to do before other things, because you want to or have to.

Your priorities are a nitty-gritty picture of how you are living out your values. If something is truly important to you, it will land high on your list of things to do, enjoy, use, etc.

One man's order of priorities made front page news late in 1977 when Jean Bedel Bokassa, a former

French paratrooper, crowned himself emperor of the Central African Republic in a ceremony that cost *30 million dollars*. As part of the festivities Bokassa received a six-foot diamond-encrusted scepter, was draped in a 24-foot red velvet cloak, and sat on a two-ton gold-plated throne, shaped like a 15-foot high eagle with an 18-foot wingspan.

Following Bokassa's coronation a gala reception for 2,000 guests included hundreds of pounds of caviar and 24,000 bottles of champagne, flown by chartered plane from Paris.

As a comparatively new nation (founded in 1960), was the Central African Republic really ready for Bokassa's 30 million dollar blowout? It wouldn't seem so. Boasting a population of two million, Bokassa's kingdom is listed as one of the world's 25 poorest countries, with an annual income of only $155 per person.[1] Yet Bokassa was quoted as saying, "One cannot create a great history without sacrifices."[2]

It would be simple enough to observe that Emperor Bokassa's priorities desperately need straightening out. Dozens of worthwhile things could have been built or purchased with the 30 million dollars. But it really doesn't help much to judge Emperor Bokassa. He is a rather extreme example of how one man set up his priorities. The question for us is: How should Christians set up *their* priorities in regard to money, time, activities? Did Jesus have anything to say about priorities? If He did, are we listening?

WHAT DID JESUS SAY ABOUT "PRIORITIES"?

If you think about it, most of Jesus' Sermon on the Mount and many of His other teachings deal with priorities. In the Beatitudes (Matt. 5:1-10) He talked about what to put first if you want to be happy.

He also talked about the importance of Christians being salt and light to the world (see Matt. 5:13-16).

He pointed out how important the law was and how He had come to fulfill it, not abolish it (see Matt. 5:17-20).

He taught us how to give the right way (see Matt. 6:1-4) and how to fast and pray (see Matt. 6:5-18).

The list goes on and on, but there is a question. What did Jesus think was top priority of all? We find the answer in Matthew 6:25-33, where He begins by saying:

> For this reason I say to you, do not be anxious for your life, as to what you shall eat, or what you shall drink; nor for your body, as to what you shall put on. Is not life more than food, and the body than clothing? Look at the birds of the air, that they do not sow, neither do they reap, nor gather into barns; and yet your heavenly Father feeds them. Are you not worth much more than they? And which of you by being anxious can add a single cubit to his life's span?
>
> And why are you anxious about clothing? Observe how the lilies of the field grow; they do not toil nor do they spin, yet I say to you that even Solomon in all his glory did not clothe himself like one of these. But if God so arrays the grass of the field, which is alive today and tomorrow is thrown into the furnace, will He not much more do so for you, O men of little faith?

*Do not be anxious then, saying, "What
shall we eat?" or, "What shall we drink?" or,
"With what shall we clothe ourselves?" For
all these things the Gentiles eagerly seek; for
your heavenly Father knows that you need all
these things (Matt. 6:25-32).*

At first glance it might seem Jesus is suggesting
that all Christians should go on welfare. Many people
honestly need welfare assistance, but there are thousands who prefer to collect their welfare checks
rather than take perfectly good jobs that are offered
to them. Jesus isn't suggesting that we become free-
loaders who don't want to work; essentially He is
saying we shouldn't *worry* about what we shall eat or
drink or about what we will wear. Worry never helps;
it doesn't add a thing and only takes away the joy in
life.

For Jesus, concentrating on material things was
definitely not a high priority. For Him the most important thing—His Top Priority—was this:

*Seek first His [God's] kingdom, and His
righteousness; and all these things shall be
added to you (Matt. 6:33).*

Because Jesus gave highest priority to seeking the
Kingdom of God and His righteousness, we should be
sure we know what He meant by these terms.

Where Is the Kingdom of God?

Scholars and theologians have written entire librar-
ies about the Kingdom, but essentially it all boils
down to one thing: the Kingdom of God is the place
where God actively reigns; where His will is done.[3]

Unfortunately, many of the Jews of Jesus' day

thought the Kingdom of God was a political one. They hated their Roman rulers, who had conquered Palestine in 64 B.C. When they talked about a Messiah, they meant a superhuman hero type who would crush the Roman forces who occupied their land and then set up a glorious reign in Israel. Jesus, however, didn't have this plan in mind at all. He claimed to be the Messiah, all right, but He planned to set up His kingdom in the hearts of those who would believe in Him.

Jesus was talking about a spiritual kingdom, not an earthly one. He was looking for subjects who would willingly seek His kingdom, enter it by faith and then obey Him as sovereign Lord. Even some of the disciples, especially Judas, really didn't understand what Jesus meant.

What Is "God's Righteousness"?

As for God's righteousness, there are two kinds. In one sense our Christian righteousness is our standing before God. God declares us righteous when we believe in Christ as Saviour (see Rom. 3:22-24; 2 Cor. 5:21).[4] So Jesus is surely encouraging His listeners to become righteous first through faith, believing and trusting God.

But in another sense, righteousness means purity of heart, doing what we know we should, being and doing right.[5] That's why Jesus said, "Blessed are those who hunger and thirst for righteousness, for they shall be satisfied" (Matt. 5:6).

To seek first the Kingdom of God and His righteousness means to try to live a holy life in accordance with God's will. Remember, however, we can't

27

live a righteous life in our own strength and strictly on our own efforts. That would be *self*-righteousness. But as we trust in Christ as Saviour and Lord, and seek to serve Him, we become righteous in practical, specific ways. Our lives will show it. That's what Paul meant when he wrote to the church at Philippi and told them to be "filled with the fruit of righteousness" (Phil. 1:11).

To sum up, when Jesus tells us to seek first the kingdom of God and His righteousness, He is not telling us how to become Christians; He is telling us how to live because we *are* Christians.[6] Perhaps a wry smile played on Jesus' lips as He finished telling His followers to not worry first about material things, but to make their spiritual condition their top priority. One possible paraphrase of Christ's words could be: "If you want to seek anything, if you want to be anxious about anything, be anxious about your soul, your nearness to God and your relationship to Him."[7] Our relationship to our heavenly Father is, without doubt, to be our top priority.

SO WHERE DO I GO FROM HERE?

Applying Jesus' words about seeking first God's kingdom and His righteousness seems simple enough, or does it? The whole issue of our personal everyday priorities suddenly looms very large. Jesus may tell us to put God first, but *do* we? One way to find out is to take a look at what really takes priority in our lives.

Try ranking the following four names in order of importance to *you*. Put a 1 by the most important, a 2 by the

28

next most important, and so on. Remember to be honest. Tell it like it is, not like you think it should be.

_____ Neil Diamond
_____ Billy Graham
_____ Donny and Marie
_____ The apostle Paul

Here is another list, with four different activities. Rate them from 1 (first) to 4 (last) in priority, according to your present life-style.
_____doing homework
_____watching TV
_____having Bible study
_____spending time with friends

Try ranking one more list, from 1 (first) to 4 (last) to identify some of your basic priorities.
Most important to me among the following are:
_____getting good grades
_____being good at what I do
_____being kind and loving
_____being popular or successful

How did that one come out? Note that there really aren't any bad choices in the list. All four are worthy objectives. But which one would be most Christian? Which one would come closest to "seeking God and His righteousness"? The Bible does not put down popularity, scholarship or success. In fact, you can find mini-formulas for achieving all of these in the book of Proverbs.[8] But the Bible has a great deal to say about being kind and loving.[9]

No matter how you "scored" on the above lists, be aware that priorities are tricky. And they vary, depending on the time and the situation. Nobody—and I mean nobody—puts God first 100 percent of the time. The only person who ever did was Jesus and He had an edge (see John 10:30).

AND WHAT CAN I DO ABOUT ALL THIS?

So far this chapter has tried to establish:

First, our priorities are a nitty-gritty picture of our values. What we choose to do, use or enjoy first is what we really value (unless we have to put certain things first due to pressure, danger, etc.).

Second, Jesus clearly taught us to put the Kingdom of God and His righteousness first in our lives (see Matt. 6:25-33).

Third, nobody bats .1000 at putting God first. Other desires and needs keep interfering.

WHAT HAPPENS IF WE FAIL TO PUT GOD FIRST?

So what should we do if we fail to always put God first? Turn in our citizenship papers for the Kingdom of God? Should we stop saying we trust Christ as Saviour and Lord and that we don't want salvation? That option doesn't look too appealing. We want to stay in God's kingdom, but does that mean we go around feeling continually guilty because we don't put Him first?

The answer is a simple no. God saves us in the first place, not because we are good enough, but because He loves and forgives us. And God continues to accept and forgive us, not because we live perfect lives, but because He is our loving Father. God knows where He is on each of our priority lists, but—wonder of wonders—that doesn't put us any lower on His priority list!

So, here is a basic plan of attack on this business of straightening out our priorities:

Start sorting out your priorities at every opportunity. What *does* come first in your life? Do your priorities ever change? If so, when? On a certain day of the week? At a certain time of year? With certain people? Why do they change?

Following is a list of 10 items that probably play a part in your life. Try ranking them from 1 to 10 in importance. Really *try*, even if you can't be absolutely sure about each choice. Tell it like it *is*, then decide on how you want it to become. What items do you want to raise higher? How do you intend to do it? What items need to be lowered? How will you do that?

____physical appearance and condition
____sports and recreation

____studying and homework

____earning or receiving money

____being organized, orderly living

____prayer, devotional life

____church program, activities

____family activities and needs

____friends and social life

____television, movies and entertainment

____witnessing, sharing my faith with non-Christians as well as Christians

____clothes, cars, the comfortable life

Stay in close touch with God through prayer to learn His priorities for your life. If you have put your faith in Christ as Saviour and Lord, you are part of God's kingdom— that place where He rules, where His will is to be done. As you are able to seek first His kingdom and His righteousness, you will be amazed at its effect on how you arrange your priorities.

At first you may not make much progress. You may get hung up on worrying about the "basics"— having enough of what you need to get by in this crazy pressure cooker world. But never give up on straightening out your priorities, on moving God up the ladder to the very top. How can you lose? You have His own promise:

MAKE GOD'S KINGDOM
AND HIS WAY OF DOING THINGS
FIRST IN YOUR LIFE
AND HE WILL GIVE YOU
EVERYTHING YOU NEED.

Chapter Three

SHOULD I OR SHOULDN'T I?

How Can I Make Better Decisions?

Decisions, decisions . . . we all face them. Some are small:

Eggs scrambled or sunnyside up? Wear the blue sweater or the gray? Go for a walk or take a nap?

Other decisions are more important:

Study for the biology test or watch TV? Take the part-time job or loaf? Go steady with Jimmie or just play the field?

Some decisions are bigger still:

Go to junior college or the "U"? Marry John or Frank? Continue to live at home or get my own apartment?

And then there are the world shakers:

Truman's decision to use the atomic bomb on Japan to end World War II; Kennedy's decision to blockade Cuba in 1962; Nixon's decision to stonewall the Watergate investigation.

Do decisions have anything to do with values? Actually, *values have everything to do with decisions.* What we think or feel is important and worthwhile affects our decisions practically every minute of the day. And how good or bad we are at making decisions has an awful lot to do with making our lives happy or unhappy, successful or frustrated, meaningful or just blah.

WHAT DID JESUS SAY ABOUT DECISION MAKING?

Jesus spoke often about the far-reaching effect of decisions. For example, the man who decides to build his house upon the sand will see it fall, but the man who builds upon the rock will see it stand, no matter how strong the storms (see Matt. 7:24-27). Jesus gave the rich young ruler the choice between keeping his riches or selling all and following Him (see Luke 18:18-24). In Matthew 6:24 He tells us we must choose; we cannot serve God and Mammon (money).

Jesus also faced decisions, and so did His disciples. One of the most dramatic decision-making episodes happened just after Jesus had performed one of His most spectacular miracles—feeding the 5,000 (see John 6:1-12).

After Jesus feeds the huge crowd on the western shore of the Sea of Galilee, the people want to make Him their king. But He slips away with His disciples and turns up the next morning on the eastern side of the lake at the synagogue in Capernaum. The crowd follows, their enthusiasm still running high. They see in Jesus the kind of leader they have been looking for. Here is a man with super powers. Not only is He a walking McDonald's, but surely He can free them from the hated rule of the Roman soldiers who occupy their land. Surely He can lead Israel back to the glorious heights it has known in the past.

Jesus faces a decision. Go along with the crowd and let them crown Him "king" or set them straight. He decides to set them straight.

In a matter of seconds Jesus pops the crowd's balloon by telling them He has not come to be their meal ticket or political leader. He has come to give them bread all right, but a different kind of bread:

> *I am the bread of life; he who comes to Me shall not hunger, and he who believes in Me shall never thirst.* (John 6:35).

The crowd doesn't understand. Isn't this fellow, Jesus, the son of Mary and Joseph? How can a common carpenter talk this way?

Jesus doesn't back off. He goes on to say:

> *I am the living bread that came down out of heaven; if any one eats this bread, he shall live forever; and the bread also which I shall give for the life of the world is My flesh* (John 6:51).

But the crowd remains puzzled. They can't understand that Jesus is talking about *spiritual* matters. They continue to think in physical terms and even speculate: "How can this man give us His flesh to eat?" (John 6:52).

So, Jesus expands His startling ideas with even more emphasis:

*Truly, truly, I say to you, unless you eat the
flesh of the Son of Man and drink His blood,
you have no life in yourselves. He who eats
My flesh and drinks My blood has eternal
life; and I will raise him up on the last day.
For My flesh is true food, and My blood is
true drink. He who eats My flesh and drinks
My blood abides in Me, and I in him. As the
living Father sent Me, and I live because of
the Father; so he who eats Me, he also shall
live because of Me* (John 6:53-57).

At this point many in the crowd have pretty well
had it. All of this "bread of life" and "eating Jesus'
flesh" talk is too much for them. They, too, make a
decision. They will abandon Jesus and not follow
Him any more (see John 6:66).

It is a tense moment. The crowd is filing out of the
synagogue. Word is already being passed in the
streets: "Forget this guy, Jesus. He is some kind of a
nut, not the one we're looking for at all."

Still standing near Jesus, however, are His 12 disciples—Peter, James, John, Andrew and the others He
handpicked to live with and learn from Him. How has
His sudden plunge in popularity affected them? What
will they decide? Jesus turns to His 12 friends and
says, in effect: "What about you? Are you dumping
me, too?" (see John 6:67).

It is the moment of decision for the 12 disciples.
They know that the tide has turned against them.
Jesus, the overnight superstar, has practically fallen
off the charts. All they can expect from here on is
second-rate billing and sleazy accommodations. No
more autograph hunters; no more oohs and ahhs

when they walk in. Instead, just sneers, jibes, quizzical looks and suspicion. Their chance to make their mark in the world has gone down the drain with one speech. If only Jesus could have been a bit more diplomatic. If only He could have watered things down, gone a bit slower with this "bread of life" approach—

But suddenly Peter speaks up. Never known for being an intellectual giant, Peter nonetheless is no spiritual pygmy. Some of what Jesus had been saying has soaked in. Peter doesn't always understand this fellow, Jesus, but there is something about Him that rings true. So Peter makes his decision and says:

> Lord, to whom shall we go? You have words of eternal life. And we have believed and have come to know that You are the Holy One of God (John 6:68,69).

If anyone among the Twelve was wavering, Peter's dramatic statement must have bolstered him. Even Judas, the one who would betray Jesus, decides to stick around to see how things will come out.

SO WHERE DO I GO FROM HERE?

Jesus and His disciples went on from that turning point at Capernaum to make many more decisions, some of which were even more difficult and complicated. Something we should always remember is that Jesus had to wrestle with decision-making just as we do. He was man as well as God. The writer of the letter to the Hebrews tells us that Jesus "did not come as an angel but as a human being . . . . He Himself has now been through suffering and temptation" (Heb. 2:16,18, *TLB*).

Jesus wasn't some kind of spiritual bionic robot who moved through life with nary a qualm or quiver. He was flesh and blood. He felt things. He made choices. He even agonized over decisions, such as the one in the Garden of Gethsemane when the thought of being crucified almost made Him want to cop out (see Matt. 26:36-46).

But Jesus didn't make decisions haphazardly. He didn't pluck the petals off daisies, nor did He play eeny-meeny-miney-mo. Jesus always based His decisions on His values. He knew what was important and what He had to do. He had His head together and knew how and why to make each decision He faced.

How Other People Affect Our Decisions

What, exactly, is involved in making decisions? Why are some people able to make decisions almost immediately, while some of us never seem to make up our minds? Why do some people seem to always make good decisions (at least things come out right for them) while others are always doing something dumb?

One group of high schoolers I talked with on several occasions thought the peer group—their friends, schoolmates, etc.—has a lot to do with making snap decisions without really thinking things through.

Jim commented: "I think it's a case of not thinking about it yourself. Instead you worry about what everyone else thinks. Suppose, for example, you're on a backpacking trip and want a little time to read the Bible. But your friends say, 'C'mon, we can go a little farther.' If you just go by what they say, you're not really deciding for yourself. Most people don't really understand what they want, because they don't think about it enough."

If you agree that Jim is right, the obvious question is, "How can we think through things a bit more carefully, in order to make better decisions?" When Jim's backpacking friends wanted to keep going, he probably didn't have much of a choice. But did that necessarily have to stop him from reading the Bible at another time? Often we have to change our plans in order to reach our goals. But how does all this work? *How* do we decide *what* to do and *when* to do it?

How to Make Decisions—It's a Process

We base our decisions on what we know so we can get what we want. When facing a fairly important decision, here are some key questions to ask:[1]

1. *What exactly is the decision I must make?* (You can't really have a decision-making situation unless you have at least two choices. Clearly identify those choices.)

2. *What is important to me?* What do I want to do, achieve or reach? (Here's where your values come into play. Different people will make different decisions, depending on what they think is important.)

3. *What do I know about this situation?* Where and how can I get more information if I need it? (Many times, *remembering* what you already know, and *thinking it through*, can save you all kinds of grief. A lot of poor decisions are made simply because people don't use the information available.)

4. *What are the risks or costs involved?* (Look at each choice available. What will happen if you

choose option X? What about option Y? What do you *value* the most? What price are you willing to pay to reach your goal?)

5. *What is my plan for carrying out this decision?* (This is critical. A lot of people make decisions and then try to "work out the details later." Often this approach leads to disaster.)

Jesus and the Decision-Making Process

Now that we have five steps for making good decisions, let's apply them to the incident at Capernaum, which cost Jesus His popularity but not His principles.

1. What was the decision Jesus faced? He could go along with the crowd and make them believe He would be a free meal ticket and maybe a super freedom fighter to boot, or He could tell them who He really was and what He had actually come to do.

2. What were Jesus' values? Obviously, He placed far more importance on the spiritual condition of the people. He wanted them to "eat His flesh and drink His blood" (be truly committed to Him), not follow Him around having picnics.

3. What information did Jesus have and what did He need? He knew why the crowd had followed Him to Capernaum—to get more bread and to crown Him a political king. He knew His real goals—to save the lost. That was all the information He really needed.

4. What were the risks? If He went along with the crowd He would compromise His principles and purpose. If He told them the truth, He would lose His popularity.

5. What was Jesus' plan? Basically, He wanted to

41

do the work He had been sent to do. After feeding the 5,000 to help convince them that He was God, He could see they had missed the point. So, He planned to set them straight at the earliest opportunity. The moment came the next day in Capernaum. Jesus' decision cost Him popularity, but it gained far more.

The Crowd and the Decision-Making Process

Now let's look at the crowd and apply five decision-making steps:

1. When Jesus told them who He really was and that free breadlines were not His style, the crowd could (a) continue to follow Jesus or (b) drop Him like a hot barley loaf.

2. What values did the crowd hold? Obviously, material things—free bread, possibly being freed from the hated Romans—were most important to them.

3. What information did they have? They had seen or at least heard about the feeding of the 5,000. Some of them had possibly seen Jesus do other miracles. They knew this man had tremendous powers.

4. What were the risks or costs involved? If the crowd stayed with Jesus, it would mean a complete change of life-style. If they deserted Him, it meant turning their backs—at least temporarily—on His offer of eternal life.

5. What was their plan? To not commit themselves to anything that meant sacrifice on their part. They always had their escape hatch ready, and when Jesus asked for their commitment they decided to retreat in a hurry: "From that time many of his disciples . . . walked no more with him" (John 6:66, *KJV*).

The Disciples and the Decision-Making Process

Finally, we have the Twelve, Jesus' handpicked companions and disciples.

1. Their decision was fairly simple: stay with Jesus, or desert with the rest of the crowd.

2. What were their values? A good question. Obviously, staying home and minding the fishing nets did not appeal to them, or they would not have followed Jesus in the first place. On the other hand, they were normal human beings. Some of them, perhaps, may have been wondering if following Jesus any farther would really be worth the trouble.

3. They knew quite a bit about Jesus. They had heard Him teach, seen Him heal and perform other miracles. They knew He was no ordinary run-of-the-synagogue rabbi or prophet. They could try to ask Him to explain His strange talk about eating His flesh and drinking His blood, but there wasn't much time. Jesus had already asked them if they had plans to leave too (see John 6:67).

4. The risks in sticking with Jesus now that His popularity had plunged were great. They would be despised, hooted, possibly even pelted by rocks or turned over to the Roman authorities as vagrants or revolutionaries. On the other hand, leaving Jesus meant cutting themselves off from the most intriguing, stimulating person they had ever met.

5. The disciples hardly had time to formulate a precise plan. Peter settled the issue for them. Perhaps Peter had planned to stick with Jesus all along and that is why, in so many words, he said, "Lord, where would we go? You are the One we have been looking for. Nothing else matters" (see John 6:68,69).

AND WHAT CAN I DO ABOUT ALL THIS?

About now you might be thinking, "Applying the five decision-making steps to a Bible story is one thing, but I've got my own problems and decisions. My life seems a lot more complicated and there are no easy pat answers."

In many respects life *is* more complicated today. Technology has "blessed" us to such an extent that we have far more things to do, people to see, and places to go than we can possibly cram into 24 hours a day or seven days a week. Life is, according to the old but still very accurate label, a rat race. Maybe that's why we need to use the five-step decision-making process every chance we get. Granted, there are many decisions that must be made quickly, in a few seconds or a few minutes. Nobody expects you to run down the list of five steps if the house is on fire or if the light just turned red. We make a lot of decisions each day that are automatic, or at least so apparently simple that we don't need a step-by-step process.

But what about the other kind of decisions—the ones where you do have two or more choices and there is some time to make up your mind?

Think of several decisions you are facing right now. Some might be long range, others may be coming up soon. For example:

• Your friend, whom you've been witnessing to, wants to go to winter camp with the church group but he won't go unless you do. You have to choose between getting him up to camp or staying home to study for a big test in biology, your toughest subject, where you must have an A to keep your grade point high enough to try for that college scholarship you want.

- Go to a small Christian college near your home on a partial academic scholarship or a large secular university several hundred miles away on a full academic scholarship that demands a B+ average through all four years of work.
- Attend a basketball tournament at the last minute with your dad (who is seldom available due to long working hours) or keep your date with your girlfriend to study for an English exam.
- Tell friends the truth about a certain person or keep quiet and let them find out for themselves.

As you apply the five steps in the decision-making process to the situations suggested above, or to situations that apply much more directly to you, here are some additional suggestions that can be of help.

First, add one more step to every decision—prayer. Jesus said, "Ask, and you will receive, that your joy may be made full" (John 16:24). First John 5:14 tells us "And this is the confidence which we have before Him, that, if we ask anything according to His will, He hears us."

Actually, prayer is something you can use in going through each of the five steps in the decision-making process.

Second, Think about how much influence the peer group has on your decisions (circle one):

a great deal   quite a bit   some   very little

Next, think about how much influence Jesus has on your decisions (circle one):

a great deal   quite a bit   some   very little

Identifying just how much Jesus Christ really influences our daily decisions can be difficult. Some days are better than others. Some situations are easier than others. One high school group I talked with the most about this book thought it was easiest to be a Christian and make Christian decisions while they were at church camp.

Randy said, "I don't know if it's just me, but have you ever been to a church camp? You get all excited and you go good for about a month and then—"

Tim observed, "It's because we spend time in the Bible at camp. If we would spend time in the Bible at home, we would be constantly that way, too."

Tim and Randy are pinpointing an experience that's familiar to many Christians. "We go to camp, a conference, or church service and we get inspired, filled, practically blessed out of our socks. And we make decisions—to accept Christ as Saviour, to rededicate our lives to Him, to read the Bible and pray more, to be nicer to our brothers and sisters, our parents, our dog. But then we go back to the daily routine and the feeling seems to fade. We go from "I'll do what you want me to do, dear Lord," to "What in the world do I do now?" All too often we forget the One who is supposed to be in charge of our lives. Instead, we think we can do our own thing, go our own way. Or worse, we don't think at all. Instead of making intelligent decisions, we just react, rely on instinct or intuition. Or, we just shuffle along with the crowd and let others make our decisions for us.

That scene in the synagogue at Capernaum has a lot to teach us. Jesus and His disciples faced the same decision: Go along with the crowd or stand fast with obedience and trust toward God? This chapter opened by observing that our values have everything to do with how we make decisions. It might be worth adding that how much we honestly value Jesus Christ in our lives will be the difference between good decisions and poor ones.

Peter, the big lovable loudmouth fisherman, had a hard time getting some things straight, but one thing Peter had very straight was just who should be at the center of his values. No matter how tightly the world tries to squeeze us into its mold, we can do no better than to say with Peter:

LORD, WHERE CAN WE TURN BUT TO YOU?
YOU OFFER ETERNAL LIFE
AND EVERYTHING ELSE WORTH HAVING.

CHAPTER FOUR

JESUS IS ALL THE WORLD TO ME?

How Can I Feel Closer to Christ?

When I surveyed several hundred high school students concerning their values, one question I asked dealt with what they would like to do, be or have. That question, containing a list of choices, appears on the next page (fig. 1). Why not check off your own answers, just for fun.

When the survey results were in, items like "have a stronger faith in God" and "feel closer to Christ" were number one in practically all groups. What makes these results really interesting is that the people surveyed were all churchgoers, members of Sunday School classes, who had gone to church anywhere from several weeks to all their lives.

Put a check by the statements that best describe you. I would like to:

_____a. have a more satisfactory life-style
_____b. not let the world squeeze me into its mold
_____c. make better decisions
_____d. be able to control my temper better
_____e. be more popular at school
_____f. have a stronger faith in God, Christ
_____g. find more meaning in life
_____h. understand the Bible better
_____i. know more about how to handle sex
_____j. learn not to waste so much of my time
_____k. know how to pick the right person to marry
_____l. live in a way that backs up my beliefs
_____m. have more dates
_____n. have a job to earn spending money
_____o. be able to communicate better with my parents
_____p. know more about what it takes to make a lasting, successful marriage
_____q. learn how to handle my feelings
_____r. feel closer to Christ
_____s. learn how to set goals and reach them
_____t. have a more effective prayer life
_____u. be a kinder, more loving person
_____v. learn more about who I really am
_____w. be sure my life will be worthwhile
_____x. be able to like myself better

Now go back over each statement you checked. Put an "X" by the top three.

Figure 1

49

On the surface these statistics might look discouraging to all the pastors, youth workers and teachers who have been involved with the teenagers who were surveyed. After all their work, these students still needed to feel closer to Jesus Christ and to have a stronger faith.

On the other hand, maybe this survey reveals something that is true of almost all followers of Jesus Christ. We value Him—to some degree or other—but we are not sure just how much. What is He really "worth" to us? Some of us feel far away from Him and we would like to be a lot closer. Some of us feel very close, and would like to be even closer. And there are probably a lot of us who don't feel He is a million miles away but He doesn't exactly seem to be next door either.

Interestingly enough, Jesus' 12 disciples had these same feelings. They lived with Him for three years. They walked the dusty roads with Him. They heard Him teach. He held special "skull sessions" just for them to explain His parables. They watched Him do miracles. He saved them from a storm on the Sea of Galilee. But even on the night before He was to die on the cross, they still didn't quite know who He was. They had just been through a very close time—the Last Supper—but their faith was still weak, their understanding a bit cloudy.

WHAT DID JESUS SAY ABOUT HIMSELF?

Some of the most amazing and mind-blowing things Jesus ever said about Himself are in the opening verses of John 14. The scene is the Upper Room where Jesus and His disciples observed the first communion service. They have eaten the bread (His body to be given for them) and they have drunk from the cup (His blood to be shed for their sins). He has washed their feet to show them what real love for one another is all about. And now He says:

> "*Let not your heart be troubled; believe in God, believe also in Me. In My Father's house are many dwelling places; if it were not so, I would have told you; for I go to prepare a place for you. And if I go and prepare a place for you, I will come again, and receive you to Myself; that where I am, there you may be also. And you know the way where I am going.*"
>
> *Thomas said to Him, "Lord, we do not know where You are going; how do we know the way?"*
>
> *Jesus said to him, "I am the way, and the truth, and the life; no one comes to the Father, but through Me"* (John 14:1-6).

To see why Jesus begins chapter 14 by saying, "Let not your heart be troubled," you have to go back to the end of chapter 13. He has just told the devoted, but overconfident, Peter that before the cock crows (before dawn comes) he will deny his Lord three times. This pronouncement had to be a downer for the disciples. Peter was their spokesman, a natural leader. If *he* was going to fail, what about *them*?[1]

Jesus senses their dismay and tells them not to worry. They believe in God, they can believe in Him. He is making reservations for them at His Father's house and someday they will live with Him there. Furthermore, they know where He is going.

51

About this time, Thomas is muttering something like, "Wait a minute, what is Jesus talking about?" Jesus is thinking of heaven, of course, but Thomas is not on His wavelength. So, he tells Jesus that (1) he and the other disciples don't even have an address for the Father's house and (2) how can they possibly know the way?

Jesus' reply makes Him one of two things. Anyone who would say, "I am the way, the truth and the life, no one comes to the Father but by me," is either someone very special, or a candidate for the cuckoo's nest.

When Jesus said, "I am the way," He didn't mean that He was going to turn into a road or a footpath. He meant something else, something every Christian should thank God for daily. It is one thing just to tell someone the way. For example, all of us know what it's like to ask directions in a strange town: "The expressway heading west? Well, you have to go down here about three blocks—no, it's four lights—at the fourth light—or is it the fifth? Never mind, you'll see this gas station on the corner. Turn left and go six more lights, then turn right, go over the bridge and double back to the stop sign. Turn right and it's three blocks to the expressway on-ramp, unless it's still closed for repairs. Then you'll have to—"

When it comes to getting to the Father's house, Jesus doesn't just tell us the way by reeling off some confusing directions. Instead He says, "Come, I'll take you to the Father's house myself. I'll walk with you. I'll lead you. I'll give you strength and guide you personally."[2]

Jesus wasn't just another teacher telling people

about a way they could get to God. He made the flat out claim that He was *the* Way—the *only* Way.

Thomas and the rest must have looked like a choir trying to hit a high note after hearing that one. But Jesus ignores their gaping mouths and goes on to say something even more staggering:

> *"If you had known Me, you would have known My Father also; from now on you know Him, and have seen Him."*
>
> *Philip said to Him, "Lord, show us the Father, and it is enough for us."*
>
> *Jesus said to him, "Have I been so long with you, and yet you have not come to know Me, Philip? He who has seen Me has seen the Father"* (John 14:7).

Jesus often spoke in parables that were hard to understand, but this time He comes right out with it and says, in effect, "You want to see God? You are looking right at Him!" *That* remark had to be even more startling than His claim to be the way, the truth and the life. Something that has always bothered people since the dawn of history is that God seems so far away. God is so awesome, so terrible, so austere and frightening. He is a ruler who is seemingly too important to bother with us, to get His hands dirty in our mundane affairs. But in Jesus Christ God came close. He entered human history. He invaded our planet. He became flesh and blood and lived among us. He dirtied His hands in more ways than one to bring us His love.

In Jesus, God loved us. In fact, He loved us so much He went to the cross. It is hard to picture an earthly ruler who would willingly do this. Kings, emperors, dictators, and others with absolute power have not been known for their self-sacrifice. In fact, they have usually been known for the opposite, especially if any of their subjects stepped out of line.

In ancient times, if the king didn't like you it could mean anything from having your eyes put out to being skinned alive or boiled in oil. During the twentieth century we have seen the work of Lenin and Stalin, communist dictators who sent millions to slavery or death in Siberia.[3] Hitler's holocaust—a maniacal attempt to exterminate the Jewish race during World War II—is forever burned into our memories.

In recent years Idi Amin, ruler of the African nation of Uganda, has murdered over 300,000 of his subjects. Bodies piled up so high they had to be buried in mass graves or tossed to the crocodiles in the Nile River. On February 18, 1977 Amin ordered hundreds of the Langi tribe (who are mostly Christians), to be clubbed or strangled to death because he thought they were plotting against him.[4]

But in Jesus we see a King who did not persecute and murder. By His own choice *He* was persecuted and murdered by those in rebellion against Him and His heavenly Father. Why? To take care of our major problem—sin. In Jesus, God Himself died for our sins, because He loved us. And He loves us still. He never gets tired of us, never gets fed up with us, always cares, always understands, always forgives when we sincerely repent and ask forgiveness.

SO WHERE DO I GO FROM HERE?

In passages like John 14 and many other places,[5] the Bible makes it clear that God lived among us.

Through Jesus we can know God *personally*. Knowing that we can become personally acquainted with God through Jesus Christ is exciting. We know God puts high value on us. But how much, really, do we value Him?

One way to find out is to take a look at just how well we know this man they called Jesus. The one who never lost His cool, never got rattled. The one who said and did wonderful things. The one who finally died on a cross and was buried in a tomb behind a gigantic stone. The one who rose from the dead and talked again with His disciples.

For example, how do you think Jesus looked? When you picture Him in your mind's eye, what do you see? (underline one):
soft white skin/ leathery suntan
sinew and muscle/ not much of a build
a loud resonant voice/ a soft but clear voice
quick energetic movements/ steady, unhurried pace

(It may be difficult to come up with a very clear idea of how Jesus looked and acted, but try putting down your ideas. For centuries a ridiculous rumor has circulated, which labels Jesus as some kind of soft, effeminate pansy. Did the first image that came to your mind give you that kind of picture, or something else?)

Now try describing Jesus as a person. Which of the following seem to fit Him best? (underline one):
a dynamic orator/a quiet confident teacher
a powerful leader/ a gentle counselor
someone you can talk to/ someone you better listen to

(Granted, choosing between some of these combinations may be difficult because sometimes both seem to fit. But try to pick the descriptions that seem most applicable, as far as you are concerned. It will help you get a sharper picture of just *who* Jesus is to *you*.)

Next, try to picture what your relationship to Jesus is really like. Pick the phrase that is most accurate for you, right now (underline one).
Walking with Christ is like:
going uphill
climbing a mountain
going downhill
uphill and downhill

Spending time with Jesus is like:
a ride in a surfer van
a ride in the family sedan
a ride in a sports car
a ride on a motorcycle

Trying to communicate with Jesus is like:
talking to the wall
chatting with a good friend
an interview with the principal
listening to your pastor
talking with an understanding counselor

Making choices like those above may be fun or frustrating. Everyone is different, with different perceptions and ideas. Maybe very few of the choices fit your own ideas of who Jesus is to you. But the thing to do is use these suggestions as starters to paint your own picture of who Jesus is to you. It may give you some clues about why you feel far from Him, close to Him, or just "in the neighborhood."

AND WHAT CAN I DO ABOUT ALL THIS?

For most of us the problem is not a need to "get away from Jesus for awhile." According to that survey I conducted, about 90 percent of the people polled wanted to get *closer* to Christ. While talking about the survey results with one group of high school students, I asked them, "Why such a high percentage who felt this need, especially when most of those polled were steady churchgoers?"

MARK: It's hard to know someone you can't see.

RANDY: I think it has to do with how we spend our time. So many things are going on in a person's life—at school and everything—and lots of times you forget about Christ because you get wrapped up in these other things.

RUTH: It's kind of like you know Him, but you don't know Him.

TIM: I think it's like Mark said. You can't see God so it's hard to develop a love for Him and feel close to Him. It's like having a good friend who moves away and you don't think of that friend as often as when you could see him. You begin thinking about yourself and other things. But if you correspond with letters and stuff, you think about each other more. It's the same way with being a Christian. If you pray and read the Bible, you will be thinking more about Him and learn to love Him.

DIANE: We seem to be talking about how to have a tangible, real relationship with an invisible, un-

HOW DO YOU HAVE A REAL RELATIONSHIP WITH AN INVISIBLE, UNHUGGABLE BEING?

touchable, unsqueezable, unhuggable being. And once you've started that, how do you keep it going? The mind seems to forget that which isn't right in front of it all the time.

TIM: That's why you have to develop a discipline, to hang on to that—

DIANE: Doesn't part of the problem lie in the fact that, with a real person, as you talk you see him smile—there is a response, body language. Part of why we don't feel closer to Christ is the absence of this immediate feedback. So, we always go around feeling like "I really ought to be doing better."

Many of us would agree with Diane—we really ought to be doing better. But how? What specific and possible steps can we take to "feel closer to Christ" ... to "have a stronger faith in God"?

Thousands of books, magazines, pamphlets and tracts have been written to describe how it's done.

Another several million sermons and devotionals have been given along the same line. Basically, they all zero in on three basic areas: the mental/spiritual; the social/spiritual; the emotional/spiritual.

The Quiet Time Connection

The mental/spiritual area has always been a problem for most, if not all, Christians. Whatever we want to call it—devotions, quiet time, Bible reading and prayer—few of us seem to pull it off consistently. We all know what it's like to vow (again) to read the Bible through in a year or to spend at least 10 minutes a day in prayer. We have great intentions, but they don't always materialize.

If our salvation really depended on how faithfully we read God's Word and talked to Him, hell would be crowded indeed. Fortunately, our salvation depends on God's grace with no strings (works on our part) attached. However, our growth (sanctification) as Christians does depend in great measure on how much input we get from God's Word. The Bible is the only real resource we have for knowing who God is, what He has done and how He wants us to live. As Jesus said, we don't live by bread alone. We need the words that come from the mouth of God (see Matt. 4:4).

There is no easy answer, but Tim's idea about keeping in touch with a friend by letter is a good one. As he says, you have to develop a discipline to hang on to (or gain) feelings of closeness to Christ. It all comes back to this business of values. If feeling closer to Christ is really important to you, then reading God's Word should be important also. Check out the following suggestions. Which one comes closest to fitting you at the moment?

For me, the most realistic approach to a quiet time (Bible reading and prayer) is:

____a few minutes once a week

____5-10 minutes at least twice a week

____10-15 minutes 3 or 4 times a week

____daily quiet time, anywhere from a few minutes to half an hour

After picking a Bible reading plan that seems to fit you, try it for a month or two. Keep a record of how well you do. Don't get discouraged if you miss now and then or have a completely zero week. Just acknowledging this to the Lord is a way to draw closer to Him. He's not asking for perfection, just your fellowship and honest commitment.

The Body Life Connection

A popular term among many Christians in recent years is "body life"—meaning the fellowship believers can have with each other. In 1 Corinthians 12 the apostle Paul talks about how all those who believe are baptized into one Body of Christ, which should function together. Being together with other Christians that you enjoy and trust is a vital way to feel closer to Christ. Every Christian needs help, support and understanding. This is especially true in high school where the peer group influence is so powerful, but adults find it just as necessary. There is no age limit on needing meaningful relationships with others who are seeking to live for Christ.

As Jesus said, "Where our treasure is, there will

our hearts be also" (see Matt. 6:21). We do what we feel is valuable and worthwhile. Take a quick inventory on your own body life connection. Is it strong, in need of Geritol, or nonexistent?

For me, meaningful interaction with other Christians means:
____church worship service
____attending Sunday School
____talking with one or two good Christian friends
____meeting regularly with a group that really cares about one another

Keep in mind that your social/spiritual needs can be much different than someone else's. Some of us like to talk and share, to open up and let it all hang out. Others are more quiet, more "inside themselves." What is important, however, is that you have some kind of Christian support system—a place, a time, a group where you feel part of something that is bigger than you are, where you draw strength from others.

The "Brother Lawrence" Connection

Perhaps the best way to feel closer to Christ is to consciously include Him in your activities through the day. Easily said, not so easily done. One way to meet your emotional/spiritual needs is to make prayer a lot more spontaneous. You need quiet times for meditation on God's Word and talking with Him, but there is no law in the Bible that says you can't send up a quick word any time of the day or night, depending on the situation. Scripture teaches us to "pray without ceasing" (1 Thess. 5:17), and you can literally do this as you make an important phone call, walk into class for the big final in chemistry or arrive late to work, just as the boss walks out of his office.

The possibilities are unlimited, but the hindrances seem to be unlimited also. It is far more natural to think about the world around you than to think about Christ. As Randy put it during one of our discussions, "Lots of times you forget about Christ because you get wrapped up in other things." Being human (the Bible calls it sinful or carnal) is far more natural than being spiritual and full of faith.

A key point to always remember is that Satan will do everything he can to keep us away from Christ. In its ultimate sense, that is what hell is all about—being separated from Christ. If we get our minds on our problems, our schedules, our plans and, above all, just on ourselves, we will forget that Jesus is as close as a quickly whispered, "Help, Lord, what do I do about *this?*"

A little book that every Christian should read several times a year is *The Practice of the Presence of God*. It was written by Nicholas Herman, who became a lay brother in a Carmelite monastery near Paris, France in 1666 and was afterwards known as "Brother Lawrence." What can such an old book have to do with feeling closer to Christ while running the twentieth-century rat race?

Everything.

Poor, uneducated, and big and clumsy to boot, Brother Lawrence spent 25 years in the monastery, where he worked mostly in the hospital kitchen. He spent endless hours peeling vegetables, scrubbing pots and pans, and doing other grubby jobs that most of us don't associate with "Ten Easy Steps to Spiritual Victory." Yet Brother Lawrence was still known throughout the monastery and far beyond for his quiet, smiling serene faith in Christ. No matter how hectic things got in that hospital kitchen (and hospital kitchens were just as busy in the 1600s as they are today), Brother Lawrence was always calm, congenial, happy and helpful.

His secret? He simply practiced the presence of God.

His "formula"? In *The Practice of the Presence of God*, you will find not a formula, but a gold mine of practical, simple ideas.

Brother Lawrence established a sense of God's presence by continually talking with Him.[6]

He confessed his failures to God, but never dwelled on them. Instead he would pray for God's forgiveness and correction, which in contemporary terms might have sounded something like this:

> *Lord, I'll continue to foul things up if you let me. You have to keep me from falling. You have to put my broken pieces back together.*[7]

He set times for private devotions but put more emphasis on developing what he called the "actual presence" of God. He made a decision to never willfully forget God and to spend his entire life in God's presence, no matter what the situation.[8]

Brother Lawrence believed that everyone is capable of practicing the presence of God ("some more, some less. He knows what we can do").[9]

He was far from perfect. For example, he knew what it was like to have his mind wander while he was praying. His remedy was simple: confess the problem, ask the Lord's forgiveness and *be brief.* Brother Lawrence was a firm believer in short prayers (the long ones only cause your mind to start wandering again!).[10]

Do Brother Lawrence's ideas sound complex and hard to understand? No, but they may sound difficult. He bores right into the heart of the whole question of feeling closer to Christ. If you want to feel close to Christ then you have to really *want to move* closer to Christ.

There is an old saying that goes something like this: "If God seems far away, guess who moved." According to Brother Lawrence, the more we move toward God, the closer we will feel. How do you move toward God? A few days before he died at the age of 80, Brother Lawrence wrote:

> *Let us seek Him often by faith. He is within us; seek Him not elsewhere . . . Let us begin to be devoted to Him in good earnest. Let us cast everything besides out of our hearts.*[11]

It is almost as if Brother Lawrence was picturing that scene following the Last Supper when Philip said to Jesus, "Show us the Father, and it is enough for us" (John 14:8). Philip wanted to see God, but what Philip didn't realize was that God was standing right in front of him. It is the same with us. We want to feel closer to Christ, and He is *already* close. He is within us. If that is worth anything, it is worth remembering daily as we practice the presence of God Himself.

**HE IS THE WAY, THE TRUTH AND THE LIFE
THERE IS NO OTHER.**

CHAPTER FIVE

How Can I Feel Good About Me?

What is the most important thing in life for most people? What is the basic driving force that motivates us, worries us, exhilarates us, or depresses us?

Perhaps it all depends on where you are on life's journey. In his book, *Is There Life After High School?*, Ralph Keyes makes a strong case for the idea that when you're in high school the thing that really matters is *status*.

Keyes devised a quiz to show the difference between status and non-status. On the status side the answers included things like:

- arriving late to class, but always able to drop just the right quip to make everyone—including the teacher—laugh

65

- breaking your leg while skiing and having everyone autograph your cast
- showing up late at the important parties
- having lots of people honk and wave when you cruise the drive-in on Saturday night

On the non-status side the answers included:

- showing up at the favorite hamburger spot on Saturday night with your parents
- having to ask the janitor to open your locker (between classes) because you forgot the combination
- making Honor Society in your junior year
- consistently arriving for class early

You may or may not agree with all of author Keyes' opinions on what brings status in high school.[1] The point is, the desire for status is a powerful drive that affects nearly everyone.

Just what is behind this drive for status? Dr. Robert Schuller, pastor of Garden Grove Community Church, Anaheim, California, suggests that what all of us want more than anything else in this world is to feel that *we are worth something*. He claims that all other drives, such as survival, pleasure or power, are only outward expressions of this need for status and self-worth—feeling good about who and what we are. What we all want, says Dr. Schuller, is *dignity*. We want to be able to know and appreciate ourselves.[2] In other words, we need self-love.

WHAT DID JESUS SAY ABOUT SELF-LOVE?

Probably the best known thing Jesus said about self-love is contained in His answer to the scribe who wanted to know, "What is the greatest commandment of all?"

66

Jesus answered in two parts. First, love the Lord your God with all your heart, soul, mind and strength. Second, love your neighbor *as you love yourself* (see Mark 12:28-31). There are two ways the Bible scholars look at what Jesus said about loving your neighbor as yourself. Some say the primary meaning is to be unselfish, to do for your neighbor what you would do for yourself (a la the Golden Rule).[3]

But a possible secondary meaning might go like this: If first we love God, that will make us more capable of loving ourselves. And if we love ourselves, then we will be able to love our neighbor as we should. If someone fails to love his neighbor as himself, he is displaying pride or selfishness that is characteristic of someone who does not have healthy self-esteem.

Healthy self-esteem produces the kind of Christian living that results in loving your neighbor as much as yourself. Poor self-esteem produces just the opposite. So, Jesus could easily have been thinking about the need for healthy feelings about your own worth and importance if you want to reach out to others with genuine love.

Healthy self-esteem has nothing to do with being proud, arrogant, or conceited. To have healthy self-esteem is to feel good about yourself in a realistic yet positive way. You realize you aren't perfect. You do not consider yourself better than others. Instead you are thankful to God for how He made you (big ears, long nose and all). You don't waste time wishing you were tall and willowy rather than short and a bit on the chunky side. You don't argue with God about

HeaLTHY SeLF-eSTeeM
MeaNS FeeLiNG GOOD
ABOUT YOURSELF iN a
ReaLiSTiC, YeT
POSiTiVe WaY

why He seemed to make so many beautiful and talented people, while He made you rather plain and average. You agree with the well-known poster that says: "God don't make no junk!"

God's Love Makes You Somebody

Self-esteem sounds like a great thing to have, so how do we get it—preferably in large doses every day? According to the teaching of Jesus Christ, the source of healthy self-esteem is God Himself. That's why His first great commandment was, "Love God with all your heart, soul, mind and strength." The reason we can reach out in love to God is that we know He first loved us (see 1 John 4:19,21).

Jesus talked a great deal about God's love and care. In Matthew 10 He gives His 12 disciples instructions before they go out on a preaching mission. He says they don't have to be afraid because:

> *Are not two sparrows sold for a cent? And
> yet not one of them will fall to the ground
> apart from your Father. But the very hairs of*

your head are all numbered. Therefore do not fear; you are of more value than many sparrows (Matt. 10:29-31).

Jesus is saying something very simple, but very important. God cares about the sparrows. He knows about every one that falls to the ground injured or dead. In fact one interpretation claims that God knows and cares every time a sparrow even lights on the ground in search of food.[4]

If God knows and cares about the sparrows, surely He cares about us. According to Jesus' own words, we are worth more to Him than many sparrows.

God Reads the Lost and Found Column

Jesus also spoke of God's love and care for all men and women when He told the parable of the Prodigal Son (see Luke 15:11-32). Since early Sunday School days we have heard about the younger of two sons who demanded his inheritance (even though his father wasn't even dead yet). The younger son left home, went through the cash in a hurry, and soon found himself feeding pigs. Realizing he was in desperate shape, he decided to go back home even if it meant punishment, the cold shoulder or a big round of "I told you so's." Instead, when he got there, his father trotted out the best calf in the herd, had him butchered and barbecued, and threw a big party in his son's honor. The older son, who had stayed home and kept his nose clean, got jealous and wanted to know why he had served faithfully for all those years but had never been given a party. The father simply said, "Look, you've always been right here with me and everything I have is yours, but your brother I had

69

given up as lost. Now he's back. He's found!"

Some Bible scholars believe the Parable of the Prodigal Son would be better named the Parable of the Loving Father. Not only does it teach that God loves you but that He forgives you as well. When you realize how much God loves you, you can only respond to Him with love in return. *God's love makes you somebody.* He is the very foundation of your self-esteem.

SO WHERE DO I GO FROM HERE?

To know that God is the foundation of our self-esteem is tremendously helpful. God is the all-powerful resource to whom we can turn to build a sound superstructure of good feelings about ourselves. But what we must remember is that there is a literal army of saboteurs who are trying to wreck our self-esteem, from the cradle through adulthood.

As Charlie Brown tells Lucy: "I hate being a nothing! I refuse to go through the rest of my life as a zero!"

"What would you like to be, Charlie Brown?" asks the ever-analytical Lucy. "A five? Or how about a twenty-six? Or a par seventy-two?"

And then Lucy has the answer: "I know what you could be, Charlie Brown ... a square root! I think you'd make a great square root, Charlie Brown."

Charlie's answer sums it up for a lot of kids (not to mention adults) who don't like being zeros, square roots or minus tens: "I can't stand it!"[5]

Where are you on the self-esteem scale right now? How much or how well do you value yourself? How well do you know yourself? The better you know yourself the more easily you can identify your good qualities and also set goals to work on your weak spots.

Following are three brief quizzes containing three questions each. In each question you mark yourself on a scale of 1 to 10. Whatever number you mark is also your "score" for that question. The three quizzes are designed to help you evaluate your self-esteem and God, your self-esteem and your personality, your self-esteem and your talents and abilities.

My self-esteem and God

1	2	3	4	5	6	7	8	9	10

I'm not sure
God values me
very much.
I goof a lot.

I'm always sure
God values me
a great deal,
even when I goof.

1	2	3	4	5	6	7	8	9	10

I have many
doubts and
I'm sure God
is not happy
with me for this.
It's a sin
to doubt.

I'm usually
very sure of
what I believe
and I know God
understands,
even when I
have doubts.

1	2	3	4	5	6	7	8	9	10

God makes a
lot of demands
and I don't always
measure up.

God forgives
and accepts me,
even though I
fail to measure up
to His standards.

Now total up your scores. If you scored 10 or lower for all three questions, the very foundation of your self-esteem—God and His love—is shaky. Look for ways to strengthen your relationship to Him. Remember that your self-esteem is based on what God—not someone else—thinks of you. If we think God is judging us on the basis of our performance, we will respond to Him with guilt, shame and fear. When our performance is weak or poor, which often happens, we will be unsure of our relationship to God and our self-esteem has to suffer. Performance oriented Christians live in a cage labeled, "God won't really accept me if I fail."[6] God accepts us because of what Jesus Christ did for us on the cross, not because of our performance.

For just a few of the many times the Bible talks about how God accepts us through the cross, see Ephesians 1:5-7; Romans 3:24-28; Galatians 3:10-13; 1 Peter 1:18-21; and Ephesians 2:8-10. If possible, read these passages in a modern translation such as *Phillips*.

If your score totals 11-20, your relationship to God may be fairly solid, or it's possible you are living in that gray neutral zone, not feeling really good or bad about God's acceptance and forgiveness. Read the verses listed above and then try writing a prayer of thanksgiving for what they mean to you.

If you scored a total of 21-30, the indications are that you and God are on very good terms. If you still tend to slip back toward feeling that you must perform to win God's favor, have the verses listed above marked in a special way in your Bible and read them often. Keep in mind that God's forgiveness and acceptance of us through Christ does not mean we should ignore His guidelines for right living. We aren't saved *by* works but we are saved *to* work, out of love and gratitude, not fear and guilt.

Now that you have looked at your self-esteem and God, try your self-esteem and your personality.

My self-esteem and my personality

1	2	3	4	5	6	7	8	9	10

I never get involved, people don't want me anyway.

I always get in on things, people welcome me to their group.

1	2	3	4	5	6	7	8	9	10

I keep everything inside, don't trust other people much.

I let everything out, have no trouble trusting others.

1	2	3	4	5	6	7	8	9	10

I am a loner, few friends, really don't like people much.

I am a mixer, have lots of friends, like people a lot.

If your total score for all three questions is 10 or less, it sounds like you are shy, passive, and don't communicate well with others. You may be on the introvert side, which means your thoughts and interests are turned inward. These characteristics can, and often do, undermine your self-esteem, because you are likely to think no one cares about you or needs you. We all need to feel that we can trust someone—parents, friends, teachers, coaches—and that they like us and respect us.

If your total score is 11-20, you are probably more typical, neither a strong introvert nor an all-out extrovert (which means your thoughts and interests are turned outward toward other people or things). You have a better chance to have good self-esteem, but a lot depends on the quality of your relationships with others. Living at a surface level (not really getting to know people nor being interested in their real needs) will not build healthy self-esteem.

If your total score is 21-30, you are definitely on the extrovert side. Ironically, this doesn't automatically guarantee high self-esteem, as many extroverts can tell you. In fact, their initiative and aggressiveness are often a cover-up for a poor self-image. Again, the quality of your relationships and your real concern for others are what help build self-esteem.

My self-esteem and my talents, abilities

1	2	3	4	5	6	7	8	9	10

I am
very lazy,
have no
ambition.

I am very
energetic,
have lots
of ambition.

1	2	3	4	5	6	7	8	9	10

I have no
talent or
ability, I'm
just sort of blah.

I have lots
of talents and
ability, what
I don't know,
I can learn.

1	2	3	4	5	6	7	8	9	10

I always fail,
I'm a total loser.

I almost
always succeed,
I'm a winner!

If your total score is 10 or lower, your self-esteem may almost be in shambles. Are you *sure* you are *that* lazy, *that* untalented, *always* a loser? Or is this just a lot of garbage certain people have been feeding you?

If your total score is 11-20 you're in that well-known average range. Your self-esteem is alive and in fairly good health, but it probably could be stronger. Are you sure you scored yourself high enough or are you trying to be "humble"?

If your total score is 21-30, you have a very good opinion of your talents and abilities, which is normally a strong builder of self-esteem. Even if you're not quite that good, the important thing is to honestly feel you are. We all live up to what is expected of us, by others or by ourselves.

Just for fun, add up your score for all three quizzes (all nine questions). If you got 30 or less, it suggests you don't feel too good about yourself. A score of 31-60 says you feel fairly good about yourself, but probably not on a consistent basis. A score of 61-90 says you usually feel very good about yourself. (If you got 90, don't tell anyone, they might come after you with the butterfly net.)

One thing to keep in mind is that quizzes like these are not precise instruments for measuring self-esteem. No quiz or test will tell you the whole story. But what you can get from those nine questions are some indicators of your relationship to God, others and yourself. And if you don't feel too good about the results, you can start thinking about ways to improve the situation.

AND WHAT CAN I DO ABOUT ALL THIS?

Healthy self-esteem is like any other form of good health. To have it, you need plenty of good nutrition and the right exercise. What you feed yourself (or allow others to feed you) is crucial. Daily workouts are also important.

In the area of self-esteem you feed yourself not food but *ideas*. If they are good, healthy ideas, your self-esteem will improve and even thrive. Feed yourself bad ideas, however, and your self-esteem will shrivel, wither and possibly die.

There are many books, seminars and courses on the market, all designed to help people gain better self-esteem. One of the best books I have found is by Dr. Ken Olson, who trained to be a clergyman and then shifted to a ministry in psychological counseling. Dr. Olson's book, which ties in nicely with biblical principles, is built on the premise that we should turn off our "negative tape recordings."

Where Do Those Negative Tapes Come From?

In *The Art of Hanging Loose in an Uptight World*, Dr. Olson claims that a major reason a lot of people are uptight, worried and lacking in self-esteem is because of the negative tapes they keep playing over and over in their heads. In other words they keep thinking negative ideas or keep telling themselves destructive things. All this is played over and over in their minds, just like a tape recording.

Dr. Olson believes that your subconscious mind is a crucial mechanism. If you continue to feed it negative thoughts you get negative results. But, if you feed your subconscious positive thoughts, you get positive results. Your subconscious mind is a powerful tool. You decide how you will use it—against yourself or for your own good.

Suzy, 18 and a drug addict, spent nine months in reform school. When Dr. Olson asked her what she had learned during that time, she replied, "You are your own bummer!" Suzy had been blaming everyone else for her problems. It was a convenient way of not admitting that no one "bummed her out" but herself. And she did it by thinking negative thoughts.[7]

We all PLAY OUR OWN KINDS OF NEGATIVE TAPES.

Negative Tapes Come in All Sizes and Colors

There are all kinds of negative tapes. Dr. Olson mentions the well-known "What if?" tapes, which thrive on fear and worry. People who play "What if?" tapes are very afraid of failure or making mistakes. They say:

"What if they don't come on time?"

"What if I drop the ball?"

"What if it rains?"

Playing "What if?" tapes keeps you nervous, up-tight and unsure. When played at their loudest, they can render you practically helpless in a crucial situation. (For example, you think, "What if I mess up this important final?" And so you do just that.)

There are many other negative tapes we could add to the list. For example:

The "I can't" tape.

The "It ain't fair" tape.

And so on, and so on, and so on . . .

How to Erase Your Negative Tapes

We all have our personal set of negative tapes. How then do we break them up? Erase them? Refuse to listen to them?

Dr. Ken Olson believes that anyone who wants to erase his negative tapes must decide that he wants to change and then takes personal responsibility for seeing that change happen. He suggests several good strategies for dealing with negative tapes.

Talk to yourself. As soon as the negative tapes start playing (as soon as you are aware you are thinking those habitual negative thoughts) don't try to ignore them. Instead, challenge them by saying something like: "I'm tired of this garbage." Or, try making fun of your negative thinking: "Yes, what if I blow it? And what if the whole world blows up?"

The idea behind talking to yourself is to make yourself self-consciously aware of the negative tape you are playing. If you are able to accomplish that, then you can also see how silly and destructive it is and deal with it. People may give you funny looks if you actually go around muttering things under your breath such as "Get outta here!" but it's better than letting those negative tapes play on in your mind uninterrupted.

Decide you are in charge. When the negative tapes start to play, ask yourself if you really want to go on feeling miserable and depressed. This is especially useful when somebody chops you low with a nasty remark. Instead of reacting in anger or embarrassment as you would like to do, try seeing the other person as someone with a serious problem. Just because he has a problem doesn't mean you have to make it yours, too.

Climb out of your rut. Don't continue in your same old patterns. Even if it feels awkward or phony, try behaving differently. For example, if you're shy, try saying hello to at least one new person each day. If you are the kind who comes on too strong, try keeping your mouth shut and letting others have their say. The important thing is to act differently even if you don't feel like it (which you probably won't). The key to getting out of a rut is wanting to, not waiting until you "feel like it." You never will feel like it; you simply have to do it.[8]

All of the above are good ideas, as far as they go.

But for the follower of Christ they don't go quite far enough. Does the Christian have any more to go on than techniques for erasing negative thoughts? For example, what can he put in their place?

How to Turn On Those Positive Tapes

There is tremendous power in what we believe. As we have seen, if we continue to let nothing but negative messages play over and over in our minds, we will believe them, and the result will be self-doubt, anxiety and low self-esteem. But positive messages—*positive tapes* if you please—do the opposite. When we play positive tapes we are more confident, able to hang loose and our self-esteem rises.

The question, of course, is how do we turn on these positive tapes? Does the Bible give the Christian any clues? Indeed it does. The apostle Paul anticipated Ken Olson's ideas on hanging loose in an uptight world when he wrote to the Philippian Christians and said:

> *Finally, brethren, whatever is true, whatever is honorable, whatever is right, whatever is pure, whatever is lovely, whatever is of good repute, if there is any excellence and if anything worthy of praise, let your mind dwell on these things* (Phil. 4:8).

Right here, in 40 clear words, Paul gives us the recipe for the kind of nutrition we should be feeding our minds every day. Paul knew that the human mind will always dwell on something. We are what we think.

For example, we should think about:

Things that are true. We don't knowingly put our

trust in the false and the phony. We want to count on the things that are reliable and accurate. Unfortunately, many Christians get sucked into believing the garbage in various kinds of negative tapes.

Sometimes the messages start in our own heads; sometimes other people lay them on us. But when you make a mistake, don't condemn yourself by saying things like, "You dummy, you always goof" or "You never do things right." Instead, say things like: "Well, I tried but I didn't quite make it." Or there's nothing wrong with going to the old cliches like, "Nobody's perfect" (nobody is) and "You can't win 'em all" (you can't). Find the truth about yourself. Don't exaggerate in either direction.

Another idea is to remind yourself of the fantastic truths in the Bible:

"Jesus does love me" (warts and all).

"God doesn't expect me to become perfect overnight" (He's very patient).

"The Holy Spirit is at work in me right now" (and He isn't going to go on strike for better conditions).

"I can do anything" (that Christ wants me to).

Things that are honest (or honorable). During the Watergate investigation there was a lot of talk about honor and dishonor. President Richard Nixon and his staff were all charged with destroying America's national honor before the eyes of the world. Even the honor of newly-appointed President Ford was questioned when he pardoned Nixon, while many on Nixon's staff had to stand trial and go to prison.

Many Americans were stunned, baffled and disillusioned by Watergate. How could a President and his staff do such a thing? Some people got acute attacks of self-righteousness. They assured themselves that *they* could never act that way.

Just how can a Christian focus in a practical way on doing what is honorable? One approach is to emphasize things that would bring you honor if they were said out loud (or even over television):

"I care about others."

"I go out of my way to help."

"I keep my word."

"I respect the feelings of other people."

What truthful things can you say about yourself that would bring you honor? Concentrate on doing those things and making them part of your life.

Things that are right—or just. We all want justice, to be treated fairly. The concept of justice is at the heart of the Golden Rule: "Just as you want men to treat you, treat them in the same way" (Luke 6:31).

When it comes to building a healthy self-esteem, be sure you are fair to yourself. Take your fair share of the blame when something goes wrong, but no more than that. To be able to admit you are wrong is a great asset, but don't turn it into a liability by confessing all the world's faults and taking them on yourself.

If you get hung up on playing negative tapes that put yourself down, you really aren't being helpful to anyone. A lot of people go around being unfair to themselves and they call it "humility." To paraphrase the Golden Rule, "Just as you believe others should be treated, be sure to treat yourself the same way" (Luke 6:31).

Things that are pure and lovely. Paul doesn't mean pure water or pure air, important as those things are. He means pure morals, pure thoughts. By "lovely"

Paul means "that which calls forth love."⁹ Hostility, vengeance, bitterness, criticism, jealousy, etc., etc., are not pure and do not call forth love. For the Christian, concentrating on "pure, lovely things" means thinking about your special uniqueness before God. Every Christian is righteous and pure in God's sight because of the tremendous price He paid through Christ's death on the cross. Next time the immoral and the unlovely come your way, just picture Christ standing there with His nail-scarred hands stretched out to you. It could be the best mind cleanser you ever used.

Things that are of good repute, excellent and worthy of praise. Obviously, negative tapes like "What if?," "It ain't fair," and "Why Try?" don't fit here. The ugly, the false, the questionable tidbit of gossip—none of these build self-esteem; they only tear it down in yourself and others. What Paul is talking about here are things which are "only fit for God to hear."¹⁰ To keep your mind centered on thoughts fit only for God seems like an impossible task, and it is. But the more the Christian can keep his mind on Christ, the closer he will come to this highest of ideals—and to higher self-esteem.

You can read books on building sound self-esteem (*The Art of Hanging Loose in an Uptight World* is only one of many good examples).¹¹ You can try to master their techniques and tips, many of which are excellent. But what the Christian has going for him is something far more powerful and effective. *The Holy Spirit of Christ lives in you* (see Rom. 8:9,16; Eph. 3:16)!

So, it doesn't matter if you are just plain ordinary

when it comes to looks or ability. It doesn't matter if you never made homecoming queen, cheerleader, or a varsity letter. It doesn't matter if the only A you ever got was in recess. It doesn't matter if your job lacks prestige or your car lacks power seats and power windows. It doesn't even matter if your parents, teachers, coaches, employers or friends are constantly on your case about something.

All of that is based on the world's system of values. The world accepts you on its terms and there are always strings (sometimes ropes) attached. The world determines your worth according to your qualities, abilities or performance. It's important to try to succeed in this world, sure, but it shouldn't be what matters most.

What does matter is succeeding at being a person who knows God through Christ. Even if you don't change all that much, even if you never "make it big," you still have God's acceptance and approval. You still have the guarantee and promise that because Somebody loves you, you are indeed *somebody*!

YOU AREN'T JUST WORTH "SOMETHING."
YOU ARE WORTH EVERYTHING,
BECAUSE GOD GAVE HIS ONLY SON FOR YOU.

CHAPTER SIX
NOTHING TO FEAR BUT DOUBT ITSELF

How Can I Have a Stronger Faith?

In the last two chapters we looked at two very important ideas: (1) how much we value God depends on how close we feel to Christ; (2) how much we value ourselves depends on how well we understand God's love for us.

So far so good.

Now all we need is the faith to make it work. Funny thing about faith. When we don't need it, we seem to have plenty. But when we run into a problem or a tough situation, our faith often seems to fade faster than a New Year's resolution.

Why is this so? Why can't we just go to our "bank

of faith" and withdraw whatever we need for the occasion? If you think about it, the major killer of faith is fear. The Bible tells us "Perfect love casts out fear" (1 John 4:18). Too often we see our imperfect fear casting out the assurance of God's love.

Remember checking off that list of statements in chapter 4 that best describe you? Most of the people I surveyed on what they wanted most, checked "Have a stronger faith in God, Christ." Perhaps you did too.

All Christians "believe," but we wish we could believe more. We are like the father of the boy possessed by a demon. The father told Christ, "If you can do anything, please help us."

"If I *can!*" replied Jesus. "All things are possible if you only believe."

"I believe," said the father. "Help me in my unbelief" (see Mark 9:14-24).

Don't you identify with that father? He wanted to believe but he still had doubts. He wanted to trust the Lord completely, but he couldn't quite put it all together. It's the same with us. We say we value God and His Son. We want to believe we can value ourselves because of what God has done for us. We want to feel free of guilt, anxiety and low self-esteem. Christ has told us we can know the truth and the truth can set us free (see John 8:32). But too often we are still hog-tied by fear, shackled by anxiety, handcuffed by worry. Let's face it. We find it easier to doubt than trust, we are more prone to panic than to stand pat with God's promises.

What can we do about this? Where does our faith, or lack of it, fit into our system of values?

WHAT DID JESUS SAY ABOUT FAITH VS. FEAR?

Again and again Jesus asked His followers to simply believe. And again and again their fears kept them from doing it. We can learn a lot about what fear does to faith by looking at the well-known report of Peter's walk on the water.

Jesus finished feeding the 5,000. Then He sent the disciples on ahead to the other side of the Sea of Galilee while He remained behind to disperse the huge crowd and spend some time alone in prayer.

Later that night the disciples are having a tough time out on the lake due to high winds and waves. Suddenly they see Jesus walking toward them on the water! They think He is a ghost and are almost ready to abandon ship, but Jesus calms them down by saying:

> *"Take courage, it is I; do not be afraid."*
> *And Peter answered Him and said, "Lord, if*
> *it is You, command me to come to You on the*
> *water." And He said, "Come!" And Peter got*
> *out of the boat, and walked on the water and*
> *came toward Jesus. But seeing the wind, he*
> *became afraid, and beginning to sink, he*
> *cried out, saying, "Lord, save me!" And*
> *immediately Jesus stretched out His hand*
> *and took hold of him, and said to him, "O*
> *you of little faith, why did you doubt?" And*
> *when they got into the boat, the wind stopped.*
> *And those who were in the boat worshiped*
> *Him, saying, "You are certainly God's Son!"*
> (Matt. 14:27-33).

This story is a perfect example of the kind of fellow Peter was—impulsive, always ready to act first and think afterwards. He just stepped out of the boat and started walking toward his Lord.

But then he started looking around at the wind and waves. The thought struck him: "*What* am I doing out here? I must be crazy!" And as fear gripped him, Peter started to sink.

What happens next shows us something else about Peter. He could get into trouble by acting on impulse, but he also knew where to go when things got tough. "Lord, save me!" is often the best prayer we can utter at certain moments, and that's exactly what Peter shouted. Jesus responded by reaching down and giving Peter a hand and a mild rebuke, "Why, Peter, did you have such little faith? Why did you doubt?"

The obvious answer is that Peter became afraid. Never did anyone start out with more faith. Never did anyone start to sink faster because of fear. A standard explanation of this story is that as long as Peter had his eyes on the Lord, he was in good shape. The minute he took his eyes off Jesus, however, and started noticing how high the waves were and how hard the wind was blowing, he was in big trouble. The same thing, goes the explanation, can happen to us today. If we take our eyes off Christ and start thinking about the situation, the details, the pressure, the problems, we go down to defeat.

The analogy is helpful, but it doesn't completely solve our problem. For one thing, as miraculous and spectacular as Peter's walk on the water was, he was looking right at Christ and he had heard Jesus say that he could come to Him on the water. And, when Peter started to sink, he could cry out to Christ Himself, reach for Christ's hand and be lifted up. In other words, Peter could exercise faith in what he could see and touch. Today, Christians must exercise faith in what they cannot see or touch. "Faith," says the writer to the Hebrews, "is the assurance of things hoped for, the conviction of things not seen" (Heb. 11:1).

So, in a way, even out there in the middle of the Sea of Galilee, without water skis, surfboard or life-jacket, Peter had it easier than we do today. What can we do then to build our faith and destroy our fears?

SO WHERE DO I GO FROM HERE?

If you could manufacture faith and sell it, you would soon have a multimillion dollar business going. Think of the possibilities. Faith in liquid form for those who needed a small glass every four hours. Faith in tiny time capsules that lasted up to 12 hours. Faith in giant mega-tablets for the really big problem or crisis.

But faith doesn't work that way. Faith isn't something we buy. It's a gift we receive and it's also something we do. Faith is *what* we believe—the truths of Scripture. Faith is *how* we believe—the degree of our ability to rest in the Lord, trust Him, hope in Him and cleave (hang on) to Him.

Take a Look at "What" You Believe

We don't have a lot of trouble with the "what" kind of faith. Or do we? Take the following quiz to get a better picture of how your faith might stand up to typical pressures today. Check the answer that comes the closest to how you would respond to each situation. Don't take a lot of time to decide which answer is the "most spiritual." Simply give your first response as honestly as you can.

Somebody comes up and asks you, "Why believe in God? What are you getting out of it?" You think:

a.____Where would I be without Him? I get everything out of it!

b.____Wonder why she's asking that? My religion is my business.

c.____I'm not sure. Wish I *knew* what I was getting out of it.

One of your instructors makes an offhand remark about Jesus Christ being a victim of the establishment, "Too bad He had to die so young before He had time to change more things." Your first thought is:

a.____Jesus *did* change things. He was God, He died for our sins.

b.____Why is he criticizing Christianity again? When Jesus died was God's business.

c.____I wonder why Jesus wasn't allowed to live longer, do more good?

An acquaintance comments: "I can't buy this 'Christ died for our sins' bit. It's too easy to just believe and be saved. You have to earn what you get in this world." Your response is to:

a.____Explain that Christ had to die for our sins because we cannot match God's standards ourselves. No one can earn his salvation, but Christians serve Christ out of love and gratitude.

b.____Tell this person he ought to try reading the Bible; then get out of there, fast.

c.____Change the subject, explaining that everyone has a right to his own beliefs.

Your pastor preaches an inspiring sermon on the value of Bible reading and study. Your response is to:

a.____Renew your determination to spend more time in Scripture.

b.____Be a little irked with your pastor for preaching the same old stuff when there are so many important issues to discuss.

c.____Yawn.

A Christian you have known for a long time surprises you by expressing doubts about the effectiveness of prayer. "Lately I pray but God just doesn't answer," Harry says. "Does it really do any good? God knows what's going to happen anyway." You think:

a.____We don't pray primarily to get answers. We pray to talk to God and share our lives with Him.

b.____What's the matter with Harry? He must be losing his faith.

c.____Now that I think of it, I have a lot of unanswered prayers. I wonder—

There are no right or wrong answers to a quiz like this. It simply describes various responses to various situations or questions. Obviously, however, the *a* answers sound more confident, more full of faith. If you honestly checked the *a* answer at least four times, your faith is in fairly good shape as far as the "what" is concerned. You have a nondefensive yet confident approach to following Christ and you have a good grasp on basic beliefs about Jesus, salvation, sin, the Bible and prayer. You may not be totally fearless, but you are trusting God to guide you.

If you checked quite a few of the *b* responses (or at least leaned that way), better stop to think. You may be a prime candidate for becoming a defensive Christian who is willing to give assent to doctrines but doesn't know how to cope with opposition and doubting. Fear can make us critical or defensive.

If you came up with several checks that were closer to the *c* category, you may have a serious problem with the amount of knowledge you have of Christianity or your understanding of the gospel. Many Christians aren't sure what they believe. Their response to pressure is one of fear, or apathy.

What About "How" You Believe?

What we believe is only part of our faith picture. *How* we believe—our actions and responses—is equally important. Try this next quiz to see where you stand on the "how" of faith.

You agree the Bible is the Christian's only real primary source of information and as a regular practice you:

a.____Seldom read it.

b.____Try to read all the newest commentaries and other Christian books to see what the outstanding authors are saying.

c.____Try to read the Bible at least several times a week.

You agree that Christ is the only answer to the world's problems and you:

a.____Seldom share your faith because you don't want to offend anyone.

b.____Try to witness to several people each day because you know you should.

c.____Try to share your faith in every way you can because you want to.

You agree that prayer is important, if not vital, to Christian living. During the week you make several important decisions, have two major disagreements with friends, and get bawled out by your parents three times and your teacher twice. As you look back on the week, what part did prayer play in what you said or did?

a.____Come to think of it, I only prayed when I got in a real spot.

b.____I tried to pray, but usually acted on my own and hoped it would work out.

c.____I usually remembered to pray, not only for guidance but to offer praise and thanksgiving.

You agree Christians should be kind and loving. Your response to others is usually based on:

a.____How they treat me.

b.____How things work out.

c.____How I can best help them.

You hear that one of your best friends said something derogatory behind your back. You decide you will:

a.____Scratch him (or her) off your list.

b.____Act as if nothing happened, but keep close tabs on this friend in the future, to see if it happens again.

c.____Confront your friend, even if it's difficult, and set things straight.

Like the first quiz, this one is set up to give you an

idea of how you might respond to certain situations or problems. In this case, however, the *c* responses are the ones that would show the most faith. If you can unhesitatingly say that your first reaction was to check four or five of the *c* answers, you are on the right track concerning the "how" end of faith. Your actions are more likely to back up what you say you believe.

If you find yourself with quite a few of the *b* responses you could be sliding into that twilight zone where your faith is something you say you believe, but seldom something you do with enthusiasm. If you serve Christ at all, it's more out of fear and guilt than love and obedience.

If several *a* responses popped up in your answers, you definitely have a problem with putting together Christian practice and principle. Go back and reexamine what you believe. Faith has to start with *what* we believe, but if the *what* doesn't affect how we live, it is little more than a head trip. On the other hand, too much *how* and not enough *what* can lead to faith that is empty or even foolish. (For example, you can try driving down a residential street at 75 m.p.h. and have "faith" nothing will happen, but the police won't be too happy.)

If our faith is to conquer our fears, we need balance between what we believe and how we live out those beliefs.

AND WHAT CAN I DO ABOUT ALL THIS?

A simple, but not simplistic, approach to building your faith is a plan developed in the book, *Recycled for Living*, by Earl G. Lee, pastor of the First Nazarene Church, Pasadena, California. Pastor Lee got his idea from Psalm 37:1-7 (note that the key words appear in caps):

FRET NOT yourself because of evildoers,
Be not envious toward wrongdoers.
For they will wither quickly like the grass,
And fade like the green herb.
TRUST in the Lord, and do good;
Dwell in the land and cultivate faithfulness.
DELIGHT yourself in the Lord;
And He will give you the desires of your heart.
COMMIT your way to the Lord,
Trust also in Him, and He will do it.
And He will bring forth your righteousness as the light,
And your judgment as the noonday.
REST in the Lord and wait patiently for Him;
Fret not yourself because of him who prospers in his way,
Because of the man who carries out wicked schemes.

As the first two words of Psalm 37:1 put it: *fret not.* Stop fussing and worrying so much. Pastor Lee compares worrying to gunning your engine while parked in neutral. You make a lot of noise and smoke but don't go anywhere. He believes that legitimate concern is something entirely different from worry. When you are rightfully concerned about something, you do something about it. You put your car in gear, so to speak, and get rolling.[1]

If you are a chronic worrier, there is no instant cure. It isn't as simple as saying, "Worry is a sin, so I guess I better stop that." People who are eaten up

THE CYCLE OF FAITH

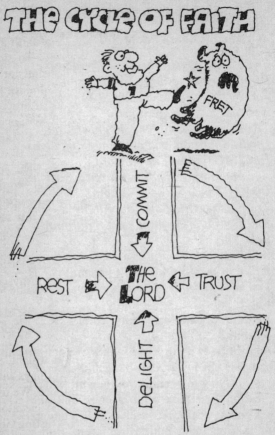

by worry would stop if they could, but they're trapped. Some of them have made such a habit of worry that they actually enjoy it in a way. At least, they prefer to worry. Others are so full of fears and anxieties they can't do anything but worry. Some of us are like Charlie Brown who told Lucy, "I worry about my worrying so much that my anxieties have anxieties."[2]

If you want to use Pastor Lee's cycle of faith approach, your first step is to stop *fretting*. To stop *fretting* you have to make a conscious decision not to let things get to you. You can do that by *committing* yourself to Christ. Yes, you have heard that one before, but Pastor Lee has a new twist. As a missionary in India, he learned the Marathi language. In Marathi, a free translation of "Commit your way to the Lord" would be "Turn what you are and what you have over to God—palms down!" In other words, don't knowingly bring along any hidden hang-ups or agendas. Whatever the problem, you don't just say, "Here, Lord, take it." Instead, you say, "Here, Lord, I let it go!" There is a big difference.[3]

Trust is the next step. Someone once asked Pastor Lee: "I've committed everything, including myself, to the Lord. Now what do I do?"

He replied, "There is only one thing to do, lean hard! . . . You don't just lean; you lean on Someone well able to carry your weight."

That "Someone well able to carry our weight" is God, but we seem to be able to trust other things with our weight more easily than we do the Lord. We use chairs, bridges, walkways, escalators and elevators with nary a qualm. But when it comes to trusting God with a problem, it seems harder.

One helpful idea came from Diane, a leader in the group I talked with as part of the research for this book. She pointed out: "Sometimes we try trusting too much at one time. For example, a little girl would probably be afraid to jump out of a 10-foot tree into her daddy's arms. But she might be willing to try jumping off a one-foot rock and let her daddy catch her. So often we hear we should trust God with everything, and I agree we should. But our faith isn't always that strong. Some of us might do better to take smaller steps of faith and work up to "everything."

Following trust comes *delight*. The psalmist tells us to delight ourselves in the Lord and He will give us what we want (see Ps. 37:4). Sounds too good to be true, and a little questionable, too. We may have heard from our pastor or other spiritual advisors that getting what you want (the desires of your heart) isn't always so good. We may want the wrong things or too much of a good thing. So, why does the psalmist give us this promise?

For one thing, if you have sincerely committed yourself to God and are trusting Him, there will be an automatic check on what you desire. As Saint Augustine put it so well: "Love God, and do as you please."

But what if things are going sour? Is the promise in Psalm 37:4 any good then? Of course. What the psalmist is saying is that we should praise God in *all* things. If we are praising God sincerely, we will find that what we have is good enough because God is with us. Praise brings joy and satisfaction, even when things aren't going all that well.

Finally, according to the cycle of faith, we are to *rest* in Christ. Does that sound like being ready for retirement or beyond? Not necessarily. We all need to rest now and then. Pastor Lee likes to use the word "cycle" when referring to living by faith, because he believes that "life actually seems to move in cycles.

It seems that we no longer handle one problem or one situation than another one rises."[4] We are tempted to fret and fume. We can decide to commit, then trust and finally delight—praise God for working in us. After all that, we have earned a little rest.

Granted, the times for rest may be brief or seemingly nonexistent. Just as an experienced runner learns to pace himself physically, we have to learn to pace ourselves spiritually. Next time things get hectic, try praying this paraphrase of Psalm 23:1:[5]

The Lord is my Pacesetter; I shall not rush.

We may be afraid, but we don't have to let fear— and fretting— immobilize us. If we are willing to try we don't have to rely solely on ourselves to make it all work. For example, suppose talking in front of people terrifies you. Don't fret about it. Commit yourself to Christ, trust Him and make a small beginning by asking simple questions. Then try giving a brief answer to a question yourself when you have a good opportunity. Later, you may find yourself making brilliant commentary on the subject at hand while the others listen attentively.

No matter what your challenge or problem is, there is no way to escape being afraid. But if there weren't something to be concerned about, then there would be no need for faith. So, stop fretting. Commit yourself to Christ. Trust Him and praise Him (fears and all). It's your choice:

FRET IT
OR
FAITH IT.

CHAPTER SEVEN

How Do I Live with My Parents?

What are the pressure points at your house? (Which, being interpreted, could read, "What do people in your family— especially your parents—do that drives you nuts?")

As I have talked with teenagers about their parents, frequent answers to the what-drives-me-nuts-most question include:

"They treat me like a child."

"They don't trust me."

"They're always on my back (or case)."

"They compare me to my brother (or sister)."

"They don't understand."

The list could go on and on and could be very specific in regard to curfew, driving the car, dating, hair style, clothing, friends, money, etc., etc.

And, of course, from the parents' side could come their answers to what drives *them* nuts:

"They want all freedom, no responsibility."

"They want to be trusted, but they do such crazy things!"

"He won't clean up his room."

"They never show any appreciation. They think I'm the maid."

"They don't understand what it takes to keep a home going."

And so the charges fly back and forth in the age-old battle of Communication Gap, as nobody on either side seems to "understand." Much has been made of the communication problem among today's teenagers and their parents. The truth is, there has always been a communication problem between teenagers and their parents (and there always will be). One way to approach this problem is to deal with it in the light of how much we really value our families.

What is your family—particularly your relationship to your parents—worth to you? For some the answer may be: "Everything. My parents are super!" For others, however, the reply might be, "Not much!" or even, "Zero!" In between these two extremes are a lot of people who feel both ways: sometimes their family is neat, at other times nauseating. A good place to test our real values is right at home— with that lovable, laughable, and sometimes ludicrous bunch called "my family."

WHAT DID JESUS SAY ABOUT FAMILY LIFE?

Jesus didn't leave us His own "short course" in

family living. But He did do and say several things that laid down principles for successful family life then—and now.

He Taught Respect and Honor for Parents

In the opening verses of Matthew 15, the Pharisees come to Jesus with an honest (not tricky) question. They are genuinely puzzled as to why Jesus' disciples don't go through all the elaborate rituals before eating, as the Pharisees would do. These rituals included a very special way of washing their hands, holding their fingers and wrists just so. Strict Jews, in fact, would go through this washing ceremony, not only before each meal but between each of the courses![1]

As part of His answer, Jesus asks the Pharisees a rather loaded question of His own:

"Tell me," replied Jesus, "why do you break God's commandment through your tradition? For God said, 'Honor thy father and thy mother,' *and* 'He that speaketh evil of father or mother, let him die the death.' *But you say that if a man tells his parents,* 'Whatever use I might have been to you is now given to God,' *then he owes no further duty to his parents. And so your tradition empties the commandment of God of all its meaning" (Matt. 15:3-6, Phillips).*

Jesus accuses the Pharisees of breaking God's commandments through their traditions because He knows about their shameful practice of refusing to help their own parents who might be in dire need. Their excuse? Everything they had was *corban*, dedicated to God. The truth, of course, was that they used

102

their money and possessions as they saw fit. But if an elderly parent asked for help, they would say, "Sorry, Dad, everything I have is officially dedicated to God and the Temple."

Jesus answered the Pharisees by exposing their hypocrisy to the clear light of day. They were neglecting a specific commandment of God (honor your father and mother) to obey a tradition of men that was not even in the Scriptures (the "law" of *corban*).[2]

There you have principle number one: Honor your father and mother. This is a good principle, but left alone it doesn't necessarily do much to help the typical teenager with his problems at home. In fact, some parents love to quote this verse as a blanket reason why teenagers should *never* challenge parental reasoning (or lack of reasoning) on *any* subject. Fortunately, Jesus did and said other things that fill in the total picture.

He Said Children Should Be Loved and Respected

In Matthew 19 are just three short verses that tell volumes about how Jesus saw the younger generation:

> *Then some children were brought to Him so that He might lay His hands on them and pray; and the disciples rebuked them. But Jesus said, "Let the children alone, and do not hinder them from coming to Me; for the kingdom of heaven belongs to such as these." And after laying His hands on them, He departed from there* (Matt. 19:13-15).

Imagine what this scene was like. Some mothers meet Jesus and His disciples and they try to bring their children to the Lord so He can touch and pray for them. These mothers have probably heard (or even seen) how Jesus heals people who are sick. Possibly some of the children are ill, or perhaps the mothers simply want Jesus to give their children His special blessing.

The disciples represent the "Don't bother me, kid, can't you see we're busy" attitude that adults often show to young people. They aren't necessarily trying to be mean. They are just preoccupied with all that is going on. Jesus' days are filled with teaching, healing and helping people. Perhaps He is extra tired and late for His next appointment to boot. The disciples are simply trying to protect their Master from "unnecessary" interference.

But Jesus doesn't see the children an unnecessary bother. In so many words He says: "Don't try to stop the children from coming to me. In fact, everyone who comes to me should come with the same kind of faith and trust that these little ones have."

In this brief scene Jesus teaches a major principle about how adults are supposed to relate to the younger generation, including teenagers. Whether you are in preschool or high school the principle Jesus teaches in this encounter is the same: adults should never brush somebody off because he or she is "just a kid." What Jesus is teaching here is that *anyone can come to Him*, especially children. In fact, He wishes adults had the same faith children have.

Jesus is saying that young people deserve the same respect and courtesy due adults, and that evens up the score concerning principles Jesus left us for happy family life. On one side we have the principle that children—including teenagers—are to obey their parents. But on the other side we have the equally strong principle that parents are to treat their children fairly and respect them as persons.

So much for some solid biblical principles on family living. But how do they all work out in the average home today where teenagers and parents live in various states of stress and strain? Just what can a teenager do when his or her parents have all the cards (i.e., all of the money and most of the power)?

SO WHERE DO I GO FROM HERE?

Many teenagers would say, "My parents won't listen. It's hopeless." Which is not entirely true. Some parents cannot or will not change. But that doesn't prevent *you* from changing. You are not responsible for changing your parents; that's their responsibility. *You are responsible for changing yourself.*

The following quizzes are designed to help you see just how you value your parents and certain aspects of your family relationships. Once you identify where you are in some of these areas, you can devise a plan of action for doing something about it. Oh yes, if everything is going okay at home for you, do these little exercises anyway. They will help you see how you can make a good thing even better.

How Well Do You Treat Your Parents?

When you're a teenager it is easy to concentrate on worrying about how your parents are treating you. Are they being fair? Are they being reasonable? Do they criticize too much? Are they always lecturing? The list is endless, but every street has two sides.

Following is a quiz to help you think about how *you* are treating your *parents*. After each question write in the word that best fits you: *always, often, sometimes, never*. A scoring code appears below.

1. I treat my parents with the same respect I have for my friends _____
2. I trust my parents' judgment _____
3. I try to act responsibly _____
4. I compliment my mother on her cooking _____
5. I ask my father for advice _____
6. I volunteer to do an extra chore _____
7. I pray for my parents _____

Scoring code—score as follows: always, 4; often, 3; sometimes, 2; never, 1. If you scored over 20 your relationship to your parents is excellent; between 15-19, your relationship is good; between 10-14, your relationship is fair, needs strengthening; below 10, you are probably on the self-centered trip. Even if your parents are unreasonable, irritable, etc., there is nothing keeping you from treating them better except your own pride. Try it, you'll be amazed with the results.

How Well Do You Communicate?

As mentioned earlier, there seems to be a communication gap between teenagers and their parents.

How would you rate yourself as a communicator? After each question write in the word that best describes your usual reaction: *always, often, sometimes, never*.
Scoring code appears on page 107.

1. I think, "Why bother to talk, nobody cares?" _____

2. I have trouble admitting I am wrong _____
3. It bugs me to have to explain where I've been _____
4. I keep my feelings to myself _____
5. When we disagree I just clam up _____
6. I get irritated when my parents disagree with me ___
7. My parents are unreasonable _____

Scoring code—Score as follows: always, 1; often, 2; sometimes, 3; never, 4. If you scored over 20 you are a willing communicator; between 15-19 you aren't doing too badly; between 10-14, you have a chip on your shoulder; below 9, you're acting pretty childish for a teenager.

Quizzes Give Only a Partial Picture

These two quizzes aren't supposed to give you a complete picture of how you relate to your parents. They can only give you some hints about your own situation. One thing you may have to do is take the quizzes with only your mother in mind, then turn around and do them in regard to your father. For some people the results could be very different. It's also possible that you could get a fairly high score, but still feel you have a real communication gap at your house. If so, go back over your answers again to see if you may want to revise some of them to get a more realistic picture.

AND WHAT CAN I DO ABOUT ALL THIS?

If you're caught in the well-known "poor me" trap, you probably won't do much. Without question, some teenagers have it really rough at home. A lot of others have situations that are far from "perfect" (whatever *that* is). So, it's easy to start playing games like, "I never get any breaks," "If only ..." or "Someday when ..." But that kind of game playing isn't worth your time. The real question is, "How much do I value my family (faults and all) and what can I do to value them even more? What can I do to let them know I appreciate them, prize them, love them?" One key way is to try to understand where your parents are coming from.

Parents Aren't as Invincible as Advertised

Parents of teenagers are often unsure of their ground because they are in the process called "de-parenting." When you were little, your parents did everything for you. Now you're at a place where you want to do everything for yourself. As they learn to de-parent, your folks are trying to choose which apron strings to cut, how much freedom and independence to give you.

DEPARENTING ISN'T easy

For many parents de-parenting is a frustrating, even frightening, business. Their "little baby" is getting away from them. They are no longer in complete control. (Sometimes they are afraid you are completely out of control!) They are afraid you will make wrong choices; they want to save you from mistakes they made.

Regardless of what you may think of your parents, keep one thing in mind: they have far more experience than you do. They know how easy it is for you to mess up your life in just a few split seconds. Yes, you know you are grown up, mature, trustworthy, practically invincible, but they see it differently, from a perspective that has anywhere from 20 to 30 more years of mileage on it.

There is an old joke that has a lot of truth in it. A man was describing his father. "When I was 17 my father was really dumb," he recalled. "When I hit my early twenties the old man seemed to pick up a little. Now that I'm almost 30, it's amazing how much Dad has learned."

The real point to that story is that *you and your parents see things from different perspectives.* There are a lot of things they would like to tell you, but either they can't find the words or the message gets garbled.

You may never be able to agree with your parents' fears, but you can respect why they have them and try to work from there.

Parents Are People Too

Parents are human beings who need the same things you do. As you already have discovered, parents are not invincible. Nor are they all wise, all powerful or all sufficient.

You may be slightly irritated by your parents, or you may be counting the days until you can leave home. But if you are a Christian, you must come to grips with a basic fact: like it or not, God gave you your parents and according to the Scriptures they are worth loving and caring about no matter *what* the situation might be.

Following are some things Jesus said that are excellent tips for spanning the communication gap at home—or anywhere else for that matter.

Cut down the complaints, or, in Jesus' words: "Don't criticize and then you won't be criticized" (Matt. 7:1, *TLB*). Many Bible versions say, "Judge not," but of course we all do. Passing judgment on others is a favorite sport that we seem to learn at an early age (often from our parents!). But firing back a salvo of criticism when one of your parents gets on your case only escalates the battle.

Here are three "de-escalators" that often take the heat out of an argument:

"You know, Mom, you may be right."

"Dad, I'll really think about what you're saying."

"I respect your opinion, but I guess I see it differently."

Refuse to retaliate. As Jesus put it: "Don't resist violence! If you are slapped on one cheek, turn the other too" (Matt. 5:39, *TLB*). To be sure, Jesus is talking mainly about physical blows—actually getting slapped around. But *verbal* punches are far more common in most families these days. A favorite way to send a verbal right-cross is with what is called a

110

A "YOU" MESSAGE PUTS THE OTHER PERSON ON THE DEFENSIVE.

AN "I" MESSAGE IS LESS APT TO DO SO.

"you" message. Parents often send "you" messages that sound like this: "*You* never think! *You* have no consideration for anyone! *You're* a total slob!" Teenagers counterpunch with their own "you" messages, such as: "*You* don't even try to understand! *You* always put me down! *You're* an old crab! *You* never do make sense."

Cure for the "you" message is the "I" message. Far better to share how you feel, but with an "I" on the front of it, not a "you." The minute a "you" is placed on the front end of a message it often puts the receiver on the defensive, particularly if the situation is tense or getting a bit warm.

For example, "I don't feel that is fair" is a lot less threatening to someone than, "You're unfair." Or, "I often feel put down" doesn't have the incendiary quality of "You always put me down!"

When getting hit with "you" messages sent by

someone else, one of the best ways to "turn the other cheek" is to send an "I" message in return.

Be a relentless forgiver. Peter asked the Lord: " 'Sir, how often should I forgive a brother who sins against me? Seven times?'

" 'No! Jesus replied, 'seventy times seven!' " (Matt. 18:21,22, *TLB*). When Peter asked Jesus if forgiving seven times was enough, he thought he was being a good guy indeed. The rabbis taught to forgive at least three times, so Peter felt extra spiritual by doubling this and adding one for good measure. But Jesus wasn't interested in rationing forgiveness in exact amounts. That's why He said we should forgive *seventy times seven.* To forgive someone 490 times for something sounds a bit ridiculous and so it would be if you were really trying to keep score. But in families especially, people shouldn't keep score on forgiving each other. When Jesus suggests forgiving someone 490 times He is saying we should forgive others on an *unlimited basis.*

There is no better place to practice unlimited forgiveness than in family relationships:

Forgive when you get in hassles over other people using your clothes.

Forgive when someone gets more attention or sympathy than you do.

Forgive when your brother or sister may get a higher allowance, a later bedtime or the car more often.

Opportunities for unlimited forgiveness are truly unlimited. If you don't forgive, you can wind up nursing a grudge. Grudges don't need nursing, they need neglecting so they will die a well-deserved premature death.

Be salt, not pepper. In Matthew 5:13 Jesus said: "You are the world's seasoning, to make it tolerable. If you lose your flavor, what will happen to the world?" *(TLB).* When it comes to helping season your family atmosphere, seek to be the right amount of salt, but avoid ego trips that make you peppery and biting to the taste. For example, cut the sarcasm, increase the compliments. There is nothing to improve communication like a little honest praise of Mom's cooking or Dad's new suit. Another good way to build better relationships is to praise attitudes and intentions. "Thanks, Mom, for trying to understand" or "Dad, I really appreciate how you trust me" are examples of comments that are sure to make you the "salt of the family" anytime.

Be a high-mileage Christian. Christ advised His listeners to the Sermon on the Mount: "And whoever shall force you to go one mile, go with him two" (Matt. 5:41). Jesus was referring specifically to the Roman soldiers' practice of forcing citizens of Israel to carry their gear or other burdens. Because the Romans ruled the land, there was nothing a Jew could do but obey. Jesus advised, however, not to just be willing to carry a burden for one mile, but offer to go two for good measure.

What does all this have to do with living in a family? For one thing it ties in closely with the idea of being a servant (see Mark 10:43). If asked to vacuum the living room, do the bedrooms too. If asked to take out the garbage, go through the house and check all the wastebaskets too. If "forced" to go to boring Uncle Ned's place on Sunday afternoon, instead of going along grudgingly and sulking silently in the corner, get involved and contribute to the conversation. Act *human* (even if you're convinced Uncle Ned is not).

Going the second mile or more is not necessarily fun but you can spread a lot of joy along the way.

Live within Christ's love. Jesus said: "When you obey me you are living in my love" (John 15:10, *TLB*). All of the other tips are wrapped up in this one. All of the other tips become only burdensome rules without Christ's love at work in your life. Communication is not just a two-way street; it's a three-way proposition. You have to be in communication with Christ in order to communicate correctly with others in your family, especially your parents. (For ideas on communicating with Christ review chapter 4.)

But You Don't Know My Parents!!!

No, I don't (and maybe I wouldn't want to). You may be able to come up with umpteen reasons why a lot of those suggestions just won't work at your house. You try the Golden Rule but your parents don't do unto you as you would like them to. You cut your criticism but they increase theirs. You try to be a servant but wind up an unthanked slave.

Another obvious protest you can make to all this idealism is that your parents should be doing all these things, too. Why should all the monkeys be on *your* back? You are the teenager, they are the adults. Must you be the parent as well as the child?

In some situations, yes. If the buck is going to stop, it will have to stop with you. If the ball is going to roll, you will have to get it going. But in a lot of other situations, parents are only waiting for a little encouragement. As already mentioned, many parents are not super towers of mature strength. Some parents are still trying to find out what they want to be when they grow up.

Even if you live in one of those seemingly rare situations where your parents have it together and are coming along nicely with the challenges of de-parenting, the above tips are very useful. If nothing else, you may want to try some of them just to show your parents that you are catching on, that all their modeling and example-setting has been worth it.

Don't fail to try some of these ideas just because they all sound so difficult. Of course they are all difficult. That's why people of every age haven't been doing so well with them. But pick one or two areas. Concentrate, maybe, on just one little thing. Ask God for strength and see what happens. If anything is worth a try, it's building a stronger family. And there is one good way to do it:

VALUE YOUR FATHER AND MOTHER
AS MUCH AS CHRIST VALUES YOU.

TIED TOGETHER OR TIED DOWN?

How Can I Get Ready for Marriage?

Have you ever wondered why marriage doesn't work better? Why so many kids have two sets of parents? (Maybe you're one of them.)

If marriage is, as the ministers say, an "institution ordained by God," why are so many marriages—even Christian ones—in trouble or, at best, dull and unhappy?

True, most high school students are not inclined at the moment toward wedlock. So why talk about it here? Because sooner or later you're likely to get married or at least consider the possibility. Some high schools are already offering courses on marriage and family. So it's not too early to ask, "What kind of a person do I want to marry?" And there are other even more pertinent questions:

"Am I becoming the kind of person who will have what it takes to make a marriage work?"

"How much will I value my marriage?"

WHAT DID JESUS SAY ABOUT MARRIAGE?

Jesus didn't give any lengthy discourses on marriage counseling, but what He did say got right to the heart of things:

> And some Pharisees came to Him, testing Him, and saying, "Is it lawful for a man to divorce his wife for any cause at all?"
>
> And He answered and said, "Have you not read, that He who created them from the beginning made them male and female, and said, 'For this cause a man shall leave his father and mother, and shall cleave to his wife; and the two shall become one flesh'? Consequently they are no more two, but one flesh. What therefore God has joined together, let no man separate . . . . And I say to you, whoever divorces his wife, except for immorality, and marries another commits adultery" (Matt. 19:3-6,9).

The first thing we need is a little background on this exchange between Jesus and the Pharisees. Matthew reports that the Pharisees came to Jesus to "test" Him (v. 3). Repeatedly they asked Jesus questions designed to trap Him. This was no exception. What they wanted to know was a major topic of debate in Israel in those days: "Is it lawful for a man to divorce his wife for any cause at all?"

The phrase "for any cause" was the trap. At that time the rabbis were divided into two schools of thought concerning divorce. One school, led by the famous rabbi named Shammai, said the only legitimate reason for divorce was adultery. The other school, led by an equally famous rabbi named Hillel, said that just about anything was sufficient cause for divorce—even burning breakfast!

By facing Jesus with this question of divorce the Pharisees were putting Him in a delicate spot. No matter how He answered, some people would disagree with Him. And if He did not go along with the liberal ideas taught by Hillel He would be bucking popular opinion.

As we saw in the chapter on decision-making, Jesus could care less about popular opinion. He cared only about the truth of God's Word. That is why He went right back to the first mention of marriage in Scripture. God, said Jesus, created man male and female (see Gen. 1:27). A man shall leave his parents and cleave to his wife. The two of them shall become as one and what God has joined no one should separate (see Gen. 2:24).

The Pharisees were hung up on the legalities of divorce. Jesus was interested in establishing the principle of marriage—two joined as one, allowing nothing to come between.

As usual, Jesus set the Pharisees straight on just what the Scriptures really say. Marriage, said Jesus, is something that should last for life and the only reason for dissolving it is unfaithfulness on the part of one or both partners. The one who commits adultery breaks the bond of one flesh, and divorce is permissible but not absolutely demanded. It is the choice of the party who has been betrayed.

With this teaching on marriage and divorce Jesus gives us tremendously high ideals at which to aim. But to try to reach them without His help is about as possible as climbing Mount Everest with two broken legs. It all boils down to a simple but very sobering thought, especially for the young person in the process of steady dating or perhaps thinking ahead to marriage. According to the clear teaching of Scriptures, marriage is supposed to be *for keeps*. To approach it with a hidden agenda or the attitude of "We'll see if it works out" is deliberate sin.[1]

SO WHERE DO I GO FROM HERE?

What about this business of "preparing for marriage"? Do you have a good idea of what you really think of marriage? What kind of values would you bring with you to the altar? Would you be willing to make a go of it no matter what, or just give it a go until it didn't work out?

Following are several brief quizzes. Some are designed to help you identify your ideas about marriage and marriage roles. Others can help you see how you are relating to people right now, when dating or in other relationships.

Marriage and the Bible

While you probably won't be getting married for several years, you already have opinions on what marriage should be and how you will approach getting married. In each question, circle the number where you feel you fall on a scale of 1 to 10.

How long should a marriage last?

1   2   3   4   5   6   7   8   9   10

As long as   Marriage is
it's good for   always forever
both parties.   no matter what.

Is divorce ever permissible?

1   2   3   4   5   6   7   8   9   10

Divorce is   Divorce is
often the   never an
only solution.   option.

Should a Christian marry a non-Christian?

1   2   3   4   5   6   7   8   9   10

If it's   Christian
really love   marriage
it doesn't   is only a
matter.   possibility for
                     two Christians.

Scoring code—answers in the 1-5 range suggest you are buying the secular world's view of marriage and divorce. Answers in the 6-10 range suggest you have a more biblical view of marriage and are willing to shoot for the high ideal Jesus sets forth in Matthew 19:3-11.

Current Relationships with the Opposite Sex

Your date life right now may be steady, frequent, seldom or zero, but everyone has a basic set of responses to others. In each question circle the number where you feel you would fall on a scale of 1 to 10. The scoring code below may give you some ideas on how to improve your dating life (or get it started).

What is the real purpose of a date?

1	2	3	4	5	6	7	8	9	10

to have
someone to
go out with

get to
know someone
I enjoy
being with

How important is sexual attractiveness on a date?

1	2	3	4	5	6	7	8	9	10

all important

not important

I date with:

1	2	3	4	5	6	7	8	9	10

whoever is
available

those who I
believe may be
part of God's
plan for me

Scoring code—answers in the 1-5 range suggest that you are still viewing dating as something to do to please yourself. Answers in the 6-10 range suggest that you are gaining a more mature view of dating and that you are more aware of being interested in the other person's feelings.

How Well Do I Communicate?

Lack of communication is one of the biggest problems anywhere—among nations, in business, on athletic teams, in marriages, when dating, among schoolmates. We just don't seem to be able to hear one another. In the questions below, circle the number where you feel you would fall on a scale of 1-10. (Apply the scoring code to whatever situation you like: your date life, getting along with friends, working for an employer, etc.)

Do you keep your feelings pretty much to yourself?

1	2	3	4	5	6	7	8	9	10

very closed,
seldom share
my real feelings

very open,
always willing
to share my
real feelings

How often do you put your foot in your mouth?

1	2	3	4	5	6	7	8	9	10

very frank,
often say
things I
shouldn't have

very tactful,
never say
unkind things

Are you a good listener?

1	2	3	4	5	6	7	8	9	10

never can
remember what
other person said,
unaware of
their feelings

always know
what other
person said,
how they feel

When you are with a date or rapping with friends, what entage of the time are you doing the talking?

1	2	3	4	5	6	7	8	9	10

I dominate
the conversation.

I try to
maintain a
balance between
talking and
listening

Do you get angry when someone disagrees with you?

1	2	3	4	5	6	7	8	9	10

almost always   never
get angry,   get angry,
find it hard   find it easy
to talk   to talk

Scoring code—answers in the 1-2-3 range suggest
poor communication habits or a lack of basic communication skills. Answers in the 4-5-6-7 range suggest you are
a fairly good communicator. (You should be able to recog-
nize areas where you know you need improvement and
plan to work on these.) Answers in the 8-9-10 range suggest you are a naturally gifted communicator. (You will
probably have to work at being patient with others who
don't have your skills.)

AND WHAT CAN I DO ABOUT ALL THIS?

Because the subject of this chapter is marriage, you
may be saying, "I can't do much. I'm not married,
and don't plan to be for quite awhile." There is, however, much you can do to *prepare* for marriage, something a lot of people could work on, if divorce
statistics are any indication. The best way you can
prepare for marriage—the closest of all relationships
—is to practice the same basic principles that build
good relationships with your friends, your dates, and
even your cranky Spanish teacher. Three of those
principles are: *caring, communicating, being constructive.*

What Does It Mean to "Care"?

To care is to put that abstract word, love, into
action. One way to say it would be: "Caring puts a

handle on love."[2] Romance and sexual attraction are obviously a part of falling in love and getting married, but *caring* is what will make the marriage go—and last.

Following are some questions to help you see how big a part caring plays in your relationships.

Do you care enough to want the best for the other person? The other person could be someone you are dating or perhaps a good friend. The point is, you value this someone a great deal, not for what you can get but for what you can give. The secular world's value system often says, "Go ahead, use the other person so you can have those things you love so much." A caring Christian loves the person, not things.

To apply this idea to dating or relationships with a close friend you can ask questions like these:

"Do I spend time with this person 'just for something to do' or because I genuinely enjoy this person's company?"

"Am I playing 'mating games' when I date, or am I trying to learn to genuinely care for others?"

Beware, though, because caring can be difficult. Sometimes (often?) when we try to care for someone it either backfires or we don't get much of a response back. It's easy to care for others when they respond in turn. We say we believe the Golden Rule—doing unto others as we would have them do unto us. Actually, life teaches us to do unto others and then wait for them to pay us back! But Jesus says to do things for others without keeping score.

Do you care enough to cooperate? That is, are you willing to give in and put the other person's interests

ahead of your own? This doesn't mean being a doormat, but it does call for empathy—putting yourself in the other person's shoes, trying to see how he or she feels. Opportunities to do this are innumerable:

When you're on a date, or planning one, let the other person suggest what to do (particularly if you are the well-organized, well-opinionated type).

Be on time—for appointments, dates, class, whatever. Stealing time from others by being fashionably (or unfashionably) late is a sure sign you are more interested in yourself than you are in them.

What Is Communication?

Real communication occurs when two parties equally respect and care for each other. They share information in such a way that they both understand what the other is saying. Talking, listening and understanding are all involved in real communication.[3]

Here are some tips to prevent "failure to communicate."

Open the lines. Make it as easy as you possibly can for others to communicate with you. Contrary to popular opinion, communication doesn't start with being willing to send messages; it starts with being willing to *receive* them. How easy is it to communicate with you, whether you're somebody's date or a lab partner in chemistry? Ask yourself these questions:

Am I touchy, irritable, easily hurt? If so, people will shy away from being honest with you. In fact, they will shy away, period.

Am I willing to admit I was wrong, that I made a mistake? Some of the hardest words for any of us to say are: "I was wrong, I'm sorry."

Do I use silence as a weapon or perhaps as a place to hide? Communication grinds to a halt in a hurry when one party clams up.

Listen up, which is probably the toughest part of communicating. We all love to send messages, but we aren't so fond of listening to messages sent to us. How do you rate as a listener?

Do I look right at my date, friend, etc., when he or she is talking to try to feel what they are saying as well as hear the words?

Do I often find myself thinking of what I'm going to say next rather than concentrating on what is being said to me? (This is particularly easy to do if you are disagreeing or arguing with somebody.)

Do I listen objectively or do I tend to read into things that are said to me? This kind of listening might be called "overlistening"—hearing more than was meant or just plain hearing a message that wasn't sent at all. For example, you have just pulled out of the driveway when your date says, "Wow! There goes a Trans Am! Aren't they great?" Instead of taking her remark as honest admiration of an expensive model sports car, you think: "So she doesn't like slumming in my dad's station wagon!" And the evening is off to less than a smooth start.

Train yourself to be a good listener. It will improve your date life, your friendships, in fact all your relationships. As the Scriptures put it, all of us should "be quick to hear (a ready listener), slow to speak, slow to take offense and to get angry" (Jas. 1:19, *Amp.*).

Construction Is Harder than Destruction

In relating to others most of us seem to come by the destructive skills—getting angry, being judgmental and critical, jealousy, pride, etc.—rather naturally. Building others up must be learned and it takes more than 10 easy lessons. For most people it's a lifetime course. Some never do too well. They often wind up in divorce court where they explain, "We just seem to be destroying each other. It's better that we split up."

What is the secret? How can we learn to be constructive—during marriage, engagement, going steady, casual dating, making friends? The principles are the same no matter what the relationships. Here are just a few key ones:

Be understanding instead of always feeling "misunderstood." The world is overpopulated with people who are "misunderstood." Their bosses are tyrants. Their teachers are sadists (who give too many tests).

Their parents are too old fashioned. Their friends are heartless phonies.

And so it goes. We all know what it's like to feel misunderstood. As I talked with one group concerning this book, the ever-smiling Michelle confessed that she often felt misunderstood and then added rather wistfully, "But I'm a real nice person . . . I'm really nice, you know . . . ?"

We all laughed with her, but I had to admit that I often say the same thing (usually under my breath of course). But what do we mean when we say, "Nobody understands me"? We may not want to face it but what we really mean is, "They don't want to see things *my way!* If only they were reasonable they would see that *I am right.* If they'll do it *my way,* everything will be fine!"

But for some strange reason these other people don't always want to do it "my way." They are unreasonable—even stubborn and unloving. So what can I do? The answer lies in a short prayer that is credited to Saint Francis of Assisi. It's a good prayer to repeat before going on a date, going to school, reporting for work—anytime you are going to be talking and relating to others: "Lord! Grant that I may seek more to understand than be understood."

Or, as Paul wrote to the Ephesian Christians: "Be patient with each other, making allowance for each other's faults . . ." (Eph. 4:2, *TLB*).

We all have faults. To understand someone is not to say, "*Now,* I see why you are such a clod!" To understand someone is to say, "I see your point. I don't agree, but I accept you anyway."

Don't wait to be understood. It may never happen.

128

Seek to understand and build a better life for everybody.[4]

Compliment instead of criticize. Being critical is one of our most natural destructive tendencies. To gripe and complain is as easy as breathing. It takes no brains, no training, no real talent. In marriages it's called "nagging" and it has been the death of more than one husband/wife relationship.

The less practice you have at nagging, griping or complaining now, the less you will do it later. Griping about how lousy the game was, how rotten the food was at the drive-in, how crummy the choir sounded, etc., etc., is a sure way to ruin a date or even a casual conversation with friends.

While criticizing is easy, paying compliments is usually more difficult. Ask yourself these questions:

When I'm on a date, or in some other situation with people I like, do I do more complimenting or criticizing?

Do I try to pay at least one person a sincere compliment each day?

Do I accept compliments gracefully or do I put the other person down by saying, "Oh, that's not really true," or "Well, it was okay, but it could have been a lot better."

The song says "What the world needs now is love, sweet love." One way to start loving others is to cut the criticism and increase the compliments. As Solomon said, "A word spoken at the right moment, how good it is!" (Prov. 15:23, *AMP*).

Play up potential, play down pigeonholes. Have you ever felt that someone "never gave you a chance"? Perhaps it is the biology teacher who had your older brother in his class until he tossed him out for too much goofing off. Your older brother was a goof-off, so the teacher pegs you the same way.

Or maybe you can remember never-giving-some-one-a-chance yourself. For example, you hear about how impossible Mrs. Smith in American Studies is, so you give her the cold shoulder for the first six weeks of the semester.

All of this is called pigeonholing—putting people in little slots where we think they fit. Another term for this is "labeling." We limit people by their past, or by what we think we know about their past. It's easy to put people in pigeonholes or slap labels on them. It's kind of fun, too. It makes us feel superior, powerful and in control. Have you ever heard yourself saying:

WE LIMIT PEOPLE WITH LABELS

"The guy is hopeless—he'll *never* change."

"You can depend on old Charlie—to foul it up."

"That's Sally for you—*always* late."

"She's very friendly to all the boys—*too* friendly!"

There's another word for labeling or pigeonholing. It's called judging, something Jesus warned against in His Sermon on the Mount:

> *Do not judge lest you be judged [pigeon-holed] yourselves. For in the way you judge, you will be judged ... and why do you look at the speck in your brother's eye, but do not notice the log that is in your own eye? ... You hypocrite, first take the log out of your own eye; and then you will see clearly enough to take the speck out of your brother's eye* (Matt. 7:1-3,5).

It's so easy to see the "specks" in what others do, say and think. We forget the "logs" in our own behavior. Psychologists tell us that it's typical to judge certain faults in others because we have those same faults ourselves, but perhaps in a different form. By nailing dating companions, friends, teammates, teachers, parents, fellow workers, etc., with their "specks" we hope to cover up our own logs.

For example, if we jump on Sally for always being late for appointments, is it because we tend to always be late ourselves with handing in assignments? If we hit our history teacher with being too rigid and legalistic is it because we aren't too forgiving or flexible at home?

But perhaps pigeonholing really isn't a problem for you. Be thankful and get to work on developing potential in the people you know fairly well. Seeing potential and giving it a chance to grow is what Christianity is all about. Even while we were sinners, God saw our potential. That's why He died for us. We are made right in God's sight by faith in His promises and we can have real peace with Him because of what Jesus did for us (see Rom. 5:1, *TLB*). God, the greatest finder and builder of potential of them all, has brought us to a special place. It's a place where we can "confidently and joyfully look forward to actually becoming all that God has had in mind for us to be" (Rom. 5:2, *TLB*).

God gave us a hand when we were helpless; He never labeled us "hopeless." As we relate to others, can we do any less?

What Your Marriage Will Be, It Is Now Becoming

There is an old saying: what you are to be, you are now becoming. And it's equally true that what your marriage will be, it is now becoming.

Marriage may be a long way off for you, but it will probably come. When it does, do you expect to magically receive what it takes to make marriage work by simply saying "I do"? A lot of people seem to tie the knot with no more understanding than that. Later, they wind up feeling tied down.

Each of us brings to a marriage or any relationship exactly who we are and no more. Then we have to put who we are with who "he" or "she" is. The result is marriage, which is: the most beautiful of relationships; the most difficult of relationships; the most basic of relationships.

When asked what He thought of divorce, Jesus didn't go into a discussion of current statistics or the prevalent pressures on the typical Palestinian home. He went all the way back to the beginning, to where God made us male and female (see Gen. 1:27); to where God directed people to grow up, leave their parents, find a mate and stick together (see Gen. 2:24). Marriage for keeps is the biblical ideal. Today's society may be dragging that ideal through the mud with two out of every four marriages ending in divorce.[5] But the biblical ideal of a lasting marriage continues to tower on high—a skyscraper penthouse looking down on all the tawdry tenements like Living Together Arrangements.

You have to decide where you will live and how you will live once you move in. The penthouse of lasting marriage has room for everyone who is willing to work hard enough to stay.

Encouragingly, teenagers are becoming aware that marriage is a lot more than moonlight and roses. Marriage also includes the hard work of controlling a Master Charge card and saying good morning to a head full of curlers or a scruffy beard and a breath badly in need of "more than a mouthwash."

In a Gallup poll taken in late 1977 one group of teenagers believed—by a ratio of two to one—that it is too easy to get divorced in the United States. This group of 1,087 teenagers felt there are several key reasons for divorce: marrying too young, infidelity, misuse of money, and *not working hard enough at the marriage.*[6]

You may be thinking, "I'm not ready to work that hard, yet!" And you probably aren't. The way to be more ready than a lot of the adults who have already messed up their marriage is to work on gaining the maturity that is needed to make matrimony terrific, not torture.

For example, go over the suggestions in this chapter. No one expects you to master all of them at one time. Some of us old married types (25 years for yours truly) are still working on most of them. The important thing, though, is to get started. Pick one or two skills, for example, caring enough to cooperate more or complimenting instead of criticizing, and work on these. And always use one other "skill" that will make all of the other things possible—prayer. Jesus tells us to ask and we will receive, to knock and the door will be opened to us, to seek and we will find (see Matt. 7:7). The ideal of lasting, happy marriage *is* reachable.

TO MAKE A GO OF ANY RELATIONSHIP CARE, COMMUNICATE, BE CONSTRUCTIVE.

CHAPTER NINE

WILL IT ALL BE WORTHWHILE?

How Can I Live a Happy Life?

What does it take to be happy?

A lot of people would like to know the answer to that one. After all, we all value being happy. In fact, some people almost make a religion out of "seeking happiness." The preachers of the happiness religion include:

TV pitchmen ("How's your love life?");

Real estate developers ("Get away to escape-country");

Politicians ("I promise cleaner air, lower taxes, higher wages and no oil spills").

And what about Christians? How does a Christian find happiness in this pressure cooker world? What is permissible and what is off limits? For example, is it wrong for Christians to buy toothpaste that gets their teeth whiter? Cars that get better gas mileage? Homes that are in escape-country? It seems that this is where we came in with chapter 1. The world squeezes us gently but firmly as it claims that *this* is what we should value; *this* is what is worthwhile; *this* is the way to be happy!

WHAT DID JESUS SAY ABOUT BEING HAPPY?

Jesus said a great deal about how to be happy, but He would have had a tough time making it in professions like advertising, sales or politics. For example, picture Jesus as a copywriter for a big advertising agency in New York. He turned in some copy on "Living the Good Life." His boss, a hard-boiled copy editor, has called Jesus in and is responding with some comments of his own.

" *'Blessed [happy] are the poor in spirit, for theirs is the kingdom of heaven.'*

"Poor in spirit? Wait a minute, Jesus, what are you talking about? Everybody's reading books on how to look out for yourself—how to win through intimidation, how to assert yourself, how to succeed. Nobody gets hired if he doesn't have any spirit! That line would go a lot better like this: 'Happy are the confident, for they will always be able to handle anything!'

" *'Blessed [happy] are those who mourn, for they shall be comforted.'*

"C'mon, Jesus, you can't mean it. Mourning is a bummer. That's why we call cemeteries 'memorial parks' and why some people get buried in their Ferraris. We want to forget mourning, deny that death

136

happened. Better to say, 'Happy are those who remember the good times and think positive thoughts!'

" '*Blessed [happy] are the meek, for they shall inherit the earth.*'

"Well, being meek and mild may be okay for a Ladies' Aid croquet match, but that's not where it's at in the real world. You've got to be tough to make it, to even survive. Some nice guys don't even finish last—they don't even finish! Better to put it like this: 'Happy are the gutsy who are willing to play for keeps, for they shall win more than they lose.'

" '*Blessed [happy] are those who hunger and thirst for righteousness, for they shall be satisfied.*'

"Jesus, you've *got* to be kidding. Righteousness went out with Watergate, Hitler's gas ovens and Benedict Arnold. Hungering and thirsting for righteousness in *this* world is a waste of time. It's dog-eat-dog, cat-mouse, whatever comes your way. You've got to be on your toes or you'll wind up on somebody's trophy room wall. In this jungle we call 'life,' it's 'Happy are the shrewd, for they are always a jump ahead of the other guy.'

" '*Blessed [happy] are the merciful, for they shall receive mercy.*'

"Well, I'll admit that sounds pretty good, Jesus, but you've gotta be careful. Once you get someone on the ropes, better to let the old killer instinct take over. After all, he'll do the same to you if he can. Free enterprise isn't built on mercy, it's built on guts, hard work and the will to succeed. Everybody's got a sob story these days, but 'Happy are the hardnosed for they won't be played for a sucker.' "

" *'Blessed [happy] are the pure in heart, for they shall see God.'*

"Here we go again, back to that goody-two-shoes stuff. *Nobody's* pure in heart, Jesus. Didn't you say yourself you came to bring all us sinners to repentance? To be pure in heart means you've got to trust people and where does *that* get you? Just ask John F. Kennedy, Abraham Lincoln, or Julius Caesar. Come to think of it, you didn't do too well trusting Judas, did you? It's a lot more realistic to say: 'Happy are those who never trust anyone, for they shall seldom be disappointed.'

" *'Blessed [happy] are the peacemakers: for they shall be called children of God.'*

"Sounds interesting, Jesus. But what we need in this world is men with conviction, men who will stand up on their hind legs and be counted. Nobody likes war but sometimes it's better than peace at any price, because the price can be too high. Today it makes more sense to say: 'Happy are those who stick to their guns and stand up for their rights for they won't get pushed around.' "

The hard-boiled copy editor sounds like he's been around the track a few times. Not exactly the type you would want for your dentist, but definitely realistic and wise to the ways of the world as it is today. But does he have the real picture of what Jesus is trying to say? Let's look again at these brief sentences by Jesus, which are called, "The Beatitudes," descriptions of supreme happiness.

Blessed Are the Poor in Spirit (Matt. 5:3)

At first glance we can understand why the copy

editor isn't too turned on by "poor in spirit." He pictures someone with no pep, no zest for life, no *gusto*! But that isn't what Jesus means at all. Nor does He mean we should lack courage or the will to succeed.

What "poor in spirit" does mean is: Be humble, willing to admit that God is very great and you are very small. You have the genuine awe and humility that comes from knowing that you need God. To realize this takes off all the pressure. You don't have to make it on your own. You don't have to produce your own self-esteem. You trust God for everything and His strength is there to draw upon. To do a little rewriting on the copy editor's cynical views: "Happy are those who know how much they need God and who are not too proud to admit it, for they will enjoy doing God's will."

Blessed Are They That Mourn (Matt. 5:4)

Our editor friend was right when he said people do

all they can to escape mourning and sadness. After all, there is too much misery in the world already; why make it sound like fun by suggesting that someone who is mourning can be happy?

But again the editor missed Jesus' meaning. The Lord isn't saying, "Now that your entire family has been wiped out by a tornado you can really celebrate!" When a loved one, close friend, respected leader, etc., dies or is in serious danger we are sad, and to be anything else would be a little sick.

So what is Jesus saying? He is speaking in spiritual terms. For the Christian to "mourn" in a spiritual sense means to *really care*, way down deep inside, about your relationship to Christ. This second Beatitude flows naturally out of the first.[1] As we become "poor in spirit" we see God's greatness and holiness and have to admit our helplessness without Him. In a word, we have to admit our sin, that we miss the mark and fall short of God's glory. This has to make us feel sorry, regretful. But how can feeling sad make us happy? Because it doesn't stop there. To feel sorry

I'VE GOT SIN-DIGESTION

HAPPY ARE THOSE WHOSE SIN MAKES THEM MISERABLE.

is to repent, a solid biblical word that isn't used so much these days. It sounds too old-fashioned, maybe "too religious." Instead, we toss God a "Sorry about that, Lord" and try to think of happier things. But to repent is to be sorry and really mean it. Repenting is not much fun but it is the way to real happiness and peace of mind. When we confess our sin to God, He helps us. He forgives us and we are comforted.

To put it in language the copy editor might better understand: "Happy is the Christian whose sin makes him miserable until he confesses it to God and is forgiven."

Blessed Are the Meek (Matt. 5:5)

Hard-boiled advertising copy editors always have a tough time with the idea of being meek. One of the modern definitions of meek is "spineless, easily imposed upon." Spineless people don't inherit the earth; they're lucky to get that cheap vase left to them by Aunt Martha. There are other definitions of meek, however, including: mild of temper, patient under

HAPPY ARE NICE GUYS FOR THEY DO FINISH FIRST— SOMETIMES.

injury, gentle and kind. And this is what Jesus has in mind. It takes plenty of backbone to be gentle, kind and patient, especially when the heat is on.

Biblically speaking, the meek person is under control. He has self control—actually Christ-control.[2] Christ provides the strength to handle frustration, unfairness, criticism and all the other problems that come our way each day.

The hardened copy editor may not agree, but according to Jesus, "Happy are the nice guys who keep their cool and are controlled by Christ, because they will have their share of finishing first."

Blessed Are They Which Do Hunger and Thirst After Righteousness (Matt. 5:6)

You can't blame our copy editor for being cynical about this one. To him, righteousness means morality, doing the right thing. Moral righteousness seems in short supply in a world full of dope pushers, terrorists, con artists, cheaters on income tax and hypocrites of all kinds, especially the kind he believes are in the church.

The Bible is certainly for morality and doing what is right, but this isn't the kind of righteousness to which Jesus is referring in this fourth Beatitude. Part of the biblical meaning of righteousness is: to be justified, declared righteous in God's sight because you believe in Christ as Saviour from sin. But Jesus has even more in mind. He's thinking of another theological mouthful—sanctification. To be sanctified means to be set apart for God and to grow more and more like Christ.

In a few words, then, to hunger and thirst for righteousness means to really want to let Christ control your life. As He takes control, being moral and doing the right thing takes care of itself.

But notice that Jesus says we should *hunger and thirst* for the righteousness He gives. When you are really hungry or thirsty, you want food and water in the worst way. You're desperate for something to eat or drink. To put it in terms the copy editor might better understand: "Happy is the Christian who is starving to know Christ better for he will have a banquet indeed!"

Blessed Are the Merciful (Matt. 5:7)

It's not too hard to understand why the copy editor is skeptical about showing mercy. *It is* a dog-eat-dog world as far as he's concerned. Practically from the cradle we are taught to compete, to outdo the other guy in the classroom, in sports, in business, in all walks of life. Nevertheless, what Jesus says about caring enough to show mercy makes good sense. We are far more likely to get mercy if we show it to others. In many places, the New Testament warns against not showing mercy or not granting forgiveness. (See for example, the Parable of the Unmerciful Servant in Matt. 18:23-35.)

The biblical word for mercy goes all the way back to a Hebrew expression which refers to the ability to get inside the other person's skin, to see with his eyes, to think with his thoughts, feel as he feels.[3] Today we call this *empathy*. No one ever showed more empathy than God did. He had mercy on us while we were helpless sinners. He sent His Son to be our Saviour. And Christ understood our problem, "Since he had the same temptations we do . . ." (Heb. 4:15, *TLB*).

The Christian is someone whc knows he is forgiven through God's grace and mercy. The Christian "knows how it is" for the other person. He can forgive and show mercy because he has been forgiven.[4] To help the skeptical copy editor understand these facts also, this Beatitude might be paraphrased to say: "Happy is the Christian! He can show mercy because he knows that in the final outcome God will show him mercy!"

Blessed Are the Pure in Heart (Matt. 5:8)

It's not hard to understand why our pessimistic copy editor says no one is pure in heart. He is right, because everyone is a sinner and if all we had to go on was our own human "goodness" our situation would be hopeless.

So what does Jesus mean? What is a pure heart and how do you get one?

First, understand that a person's "heart" is not the muscle that pumps blood. Biblically speaking, your heart is the center of your being. It involves your brain, your mind, your will, your soul. Your heart is the total you.[5]

Second, to be pure in heart means to cut the hypocrisy. It means having a single purpose and direction, not being double minded and unstable (see Jas. 1:8). We talk about "getting our act together," "putting it all together" and "being together." The psalmist prayed and asked God to "unite my heart to fear Thy name" (Ps. 86:11). In other words he was asking God to help him get it together. He wanted to center his life on the Lord.

144

I'M OK. HE'S OK. IT'S ALL OK!

HAPPY ARE THOSE WHO HAVE IT ALTOGETHER.

Third, pureness of heart certainly suggests being clean. David prayed, "Create in me a clean heart, O God" (Ps. 51:10). At the time he really needed one. The prophet Nathan had just nailed him about his sin of adultery with Bathsheba and the murder of her husband, Uriah. There is no way to cleanse your own heart. Only the Holy Spirit can do it. That's why David also prayed "Take not thy Holy Spirit from me" (Ps. 51:11, *KJV*).

Fourth, if we are pure in heart we shall see God. We don't deserve to see God, but we will if we let Christ help us put our lives in order.

To help our copy editor friend be a little more optimistic, the sixth Beatitude could be put in these terms: "Happy is the Christian whose life is together and centered on Christ, for he will know that God is very close."

Blessed Are the Peacemakers (Matt. 5:9)

A man of the world, such as our copy editor friend, is caught in a dilemma when it comes to peace. He wants world peace all right and he hopes the diplomats can keep everybody's trigger finger off the H-Bomb buttons. But on a personal basis, things are different. He wants to stick up for his rights, not get walked on. He wants to stand for his convictions.

But, "standing for convictions and rights" is often done selfishly or greedily. As James says: "What causes fights and quarrels among you? Don't they come from your desires that battle within you? " (Jas. 4:1, *NIV*). Jesus says we will be happier if we strive to make peace. As the old saying puts it, "The way of the peacemaker is hard," but to be a war maker is easy. A little dig here, a little chop there and you can have the place in an uproar, all the while acting under the guise of "only protecting my rights!"

To strive for peace, however, means more than just being passive, just being a good guy who "won't make a big thing out of it." Peacemaking also involves actively going out of your way to make things right.

Remember, it takes more power to make peace than it does to make war. The truly powerful person is usually the meek and gentle person who chooses his words carefully. The truly powerful person doesn't have to scream to get people to listen.

Who are the peacemakers at your house? In your school? Where you work? It takes two to make war, only one to make peace.

That copy editor who wants to stand up for his rights might better understand Jesus if the seventh Beatitude was put like this: 'Happy is the Christian who makes peace not by giving in, but by giving himself to others. For he will be recognized as one of God's family."

No, Jesus wouldn't have made it working for the worldly-wise copy editor, but then the copy editor's attitude toward life wouldn't get him a front row seat in the Kingdom of God either. It seems to be a question of values. In these seven Beatitudes (we'll talk about the other two later) the Lord turns the world's value system right on its ear. Happiness isn't something you can buy, sell, find or manufacture. Happiness, says Jesus, lies in first being aware of your real needs—admitting you are poor in spirit, feeling truly sorry (mourning) because of your sin and becoming meek (gentle) because you realize how self-centered you really are. The answer to these needs is to hunger and thirst for righteousness and then you will be filled with God's strength and power. And as a result of being filled you become merciful, pure in heart and a peacemaker.

You may want to take a breather right here to let some of these ideas sink in. The Beatitudes are not an easy road to happiness but that's the route Jesus is taking. And He's asking us, "Going my way?"

SO WHERE DO I GO FROM HERE?

No question about it. The Beatitudes are awesome. They rise out of the Bible like a 25,000-foot Himalayan mountain range—jagged peaks of perfection that soar hopelessly out of our reach. Remember the high school senior who said he wanted nothing to do with comparing Jesus' values to his own? He was afraid that doing so would make him feel guilty. After reading the Beatitudes and seeing what they really mean, we can understand why!

One thing saves us from giving up. When Jesus

taught the Beatitudes He gave us goals to shoot at, not a state of perfection we must achieve overnight or else. How much the Beatitudes become part of our experience and how happy we are as we incorporate them into our lives depends on our values, which are always under construction. The following Beatitudes inventory gives you a workable way to see how well you are adapting Jesus' plan for happiness.

After each statement put in the number that matches the word best describing your attitude or actions at the present time. 1, Never; 2, Rarely; 3, Occasionally; 4, Sometimes; 5, Frequently; 6, Usually; 7, Always.

Happy are the poor in spirit
1. I think about how helpless I am without God _____
2. God is at the center of my life _____
3. Others consider me a humble person _____

Happy are those who mourn
1. I get very upset when I sin _____
2. Repentance is part of my life _____
3. When I sin my attitude is "Sorry about that, Lord"__

Happy are the meek (gentle)
1. People consider me a meek person _____
2. I lose my temper _____
3. I try to be patient _____

Happy are those who hunger and thirst for righteousness
1. I am growing in Christ _____
2. I act like a hypocrite _____
3. I feel I am right with God _____

Happy are the merciful
1. I am very competitive _____
2. I have the killer instinct _____
3. I can put myself in the other person's shoes _____

Happy are the pure in heart
1. Jesus helps me "get it together" _____
2. Serving Christ is what I want to do _____
3. My life needs straightening out _____

Happy are the peacemakers
1. I am known for standing up for my rights _____
2. I make no trouble for anyone _____
3. I make an effort to make peace _____

Now go back over your answers. Sometimes you may have answered somewhere between 1 and 4 when you know it should have been somewhere between 5 and 7. Sometimes the better answer would have been between 5 and 7 and you may have been down between 1 and 4. It depends on how the question is worded. The purpose of this Beatitudes Inventory is to help you identify just where you stand in regard to what Jesus taught and how important these teachings should be in your life. Which Beatitudes do you want to work on? How do you intend to go about it?

It's probably better to say you don't "work" on the Beatitudes, you let the Beatitudes work on you. More correctly, you let Christ work in your life. Scripture tells us God is at work in us "to will and to work for His good pleasure" (Phil. 2:13), but He doesn't make many changes without our permission or cooperation. Sometimes God picks us up by the "scruff of the neck," so to speak, and gives us a good shake, but usually His method is to work slowly according to how much we are willing to let Him change us.

Jesus gave us the Beatitudes to help us see where we are and how far we have to grow. The Beatitudes are not just for a special few who qualify to wear the title "Super Spiritual." *The Beatitudes are for every Christian.* Every Christian is supposed to be like this, *no matter how long it takes.* And the more a Christian is like this, the happier and more worthwhile his or her life will be.

AND WHAT CAN I DO ABOUT ALL THIS?

The questions we are trying to answer in this chapter are:

How can I be sure my life will be worthwhile?

How can I live a happy life?

With the Beatitudes in the background to draw from as we need them, let's try to answer these two giant questions by asking two smaller ones:

What is my purpose?

What are my goals?

What Is My Major Purpose in Life?

When trying to identify something as big as "my major purpose in life" it helps to understand that a purpose is not the same as a goal. Goals are specific objectives, such as "getting three A's this semester or making first string on the basketball team." Purposes, however, are broader and more general.[6] A purpose can be a guiding principle for actions toward others, such as, "to bring happiness to everyone I can." A purpose could also incorporate a quality of character you want to develop, such as "being a loving person" or "being a good listener."

If you're a Christian in high school, what should be your major purpose in life? If you ask this kind of question in your Sunday School class you will probably get answers like: "to glorify God," "to be a dedicated disciple," "to serve Christ." All of these are excellent purposes, but we are not always clear about *how* they will be achieved. In the fourth Beatitude however, Jesus puts it all into a little sharper focus when He tells us that if we hunger and thirst after righteousness we will be filled.

We know that God says we are "righteous" because we have believed in Christ as Saviour. Being justified—being made righteous by faith—is a key Christian truth. But if we are honest we must admit that there is a gap between what God says we are and how we perform. God declares us righteous and as far as He's concerned, that's that. But the rub is that we don't always feel so righteous. That's why Christians may complain of empty lives, deadness in their faith, or that "church is a drag."

What's the answer to this dilemma? A major part of it is to have our purpose as Christians clearly in focus and to *keep it that way*. If we hunger and thirst for righteousness, says Jesus, our lives won't feel empty, our faith will feel alive and church will be more interesting. Call it "growing in Christ," "becoming more like Jesus," or "Christian maturity," it all adds up to a genuine desire to let God work in your life.

In checking your purpose as a Christian, ask,

"Where am I going? What does God want to do through me?"

What Are My Goals?

When you set goals you get down to the nitty-gritty. A goal is something you can measure, something you can look back on and say, "I made it!" or "Better luck next time." Goals can be rather minor things and very short range. For example, one high school student's goals for one day might be:

- Catch the 8:10 bus for school.
- Turn in the book report due in third period English.
- Eat lunch with Bill and Harry.
- Do 40 chair push-ups in gym class.
- Meet Mary at the corner drive-in for a Coke at 3:00.

Longer-range goals can be set for anywhere from several weeks to several months in advance. For example:

- Earning at least three A's for the semester.
- Earning an A in physics.
- Reading five books for extra credit in history class.
- Becoming the number one singles player on the tennis team.
- Finish sewing a new dress by the end of the month.

It's easy to see that our lives can be filled with all kinds of goals. Some are forced on us, by teachers and coaches, for example, but we should be setting certain goals for ourselves. A look at our goals tells us quickly how we are using our time and how we see life. It will also give us some good indicators concerning how happy we are, how worthwhile we think life is right now.

It doesn't take a genius to see that if you "aim at nothing you will be sure to hit it." Set no goals of your own and you will drift through life letting teachers, parents, employers, etc., set all your goals for you. It's a sign of maturity when a person starts setting his own goals and doing something to reach them.

A Beatitudes Experiment

According to Jesus we will be blessed (happy) as the Beatitudes become part of our own experience. Here's one way to take specific action to make them happen:

Step One: Make a special promise to Christ.

Step Two: Write that promise down.

Step Three: Keep that promise by doing it for 10 days in a row.

It doesn't matter if your promise isn't something heaven-shaking in scope. Just be sure it takes you in the direction you want to go (the same way Christ is traveling) and that you will be sure to carry it out for 10 days.

As you've already probably guessed, making a promise is the same thing as setting a goal. So, see what kind of goals you can come up with that are related to developing humility, genuine repentance for sin, meekness and gentleness, a hunger and thirst for righteousness, a merciful spirit, purity of heart, or the ability to be a peacemaker. Some starter ideas include:

Pray daily asking God to make you more sensitive to sin and being sorry when you slip up.

Read a chapter in the book of Proverbs each day and write down one thing you learn.

Work on being meek (Christ controlled) while talking with your parents, brothers and sisters, friends. (Even if you blow it and lose your temper the goal is to consciously *try*.)

Pick a different Beatitude each day and paraphrase it (write it in your own words).

Develop greater humility by doing something each day that combats false pride. Examples: admit you're wrong, say you're sorry, or go out of your way to help or serve someone.

Develop a greater sensitivity to sin by looking back on each day and confessing to God your sins of the tongue—unkind remarks, gossip, anger, etc.

Whatever promise you make, it is vital that you keep it. A promise kept is a powerful weapon that gives you more confidence, more power to grow in your Christian walk. But a promise broken will erode your confidence and discourage you. If you do happen to fail in your 10-day commitment, *don't give up*. Confess it, forget about it, and *try again*.

Blessed Are the Persecuted?

No question about it, a Christian should never run out of specific goals that help him or her grow spiritually. God gives each of us the responsibility to set spiritual goals. And as you set these spiritual goals, don't be surprised if the eighth and ninth Beatitudes become part of your life as well:

> *Blessed are those who have been persecuted for the sake of righteousness, for theirs is the kingdom of heaven.*

Blessed are you when men revile you, and persecute you, and say all kinds of evil against you falsely, on account of Me (Matt. 5:10,11).

The early Christians went through incredible and horrible persecution: becoming lunch for the lions, being burned at the stake or made into torches to light Nero's gardens. In less severe cases they could be fired from their jobs or lose all the customers.

Today most Christians are not persecuted in such a drastic way. But living for Christ can still run you smack into the world's value system. And when that happens you can expect misunderstanding, anger, mockery, derision and snide remarks. Why then does Jesus say the Christian who is persecuted will be happy? Because he or she will be living according to the Lord's value system, not the world's. A good way to test just how committed you are to Christ is to ask yourself: "What is Jesus worth to me? How much am I willing to take (or give up) for His sake?"

What Is a Happy Worthwhile Life?

The complete answer to that one may take you many years to discover, but you have two good clues if you can say:

My life purpose is to grow in Christ, to let God work in my life as I glorify Him.

I am setting and reaching spiritual goals through Christ.

Life has much to offer and it is often hard to decide what's really important. But the crucial key is to put Christ first and let everything else follow as He directs. Jesus said as much when He said:

If anyone wants to follow in my footsteps he must give up all right to himself, take up his cross and follow me. For the man who wants to save his life will lose it; but the man who loses his life for my sake will find it. For what good is it for a man to gain the whole world at the price of his own soul? What could a man offer to buy back his soul once he had lost it? (Matt. 16:24–28, Phillips).

That is Jesus' final word on values. It is our final word also.

HAPPY IS THE CHRISTIAN
WHO VALUES CHRIST ABOVE ALL
FOR HE WILL ALWAYS KNOW
WHAT IS REALLY IMPORTANT
AND HE WILL NEVER GIVE UP
THE THINGS THAT ARE.

NOTES

Introduction

1. Cathleen Decker, "Vendor Shot, Bystanders Loot His Ice Cream Truck," *Los Angeles Times*, February 22, 1978, Part I, p. 3.

Chapter 1

1. See Romans 12:2, J.B. Phillips, *The New Testament in Modern English* (New York: Macmillan Publishing Company, 1958).
2. D. Martyn Lloyd-Jones, *Studies in the Sermon on the Mount* (Grand Rapids: Wm. B. Eerdmans Publishing Co., n.d.), p. 79ff.
3. William Barclay, *The Gospel of Matthew*, The Daily Study Bible (Edinburgh: The Saint Andrew Press, 1956), v. 1, pp. 241,242.
4. *The Los Angeles Times*, November 29, 1977.
5. *The Hollywood Free Paper*, April 1977, p. 4.
6. Barclay, *Matthew*, v. 1, p. 244.
7. Barclay, *Matthew*, v. 1, p. 52.
8. Simeon Stylites. Simeon Stylites was a fifth century saint who was called the father of the pillar saints. At 16, he entered a monastery. Because his many duties deprived him of time for personal devotion, he began sitting on a nine-foot high pillar. He raised the height of the pillar until the platform, which was three feet in diameter, reached to 50 feet.

Chapter 2

1. "Emperor Crowns Himself in Poverty-Stricken Land," *Los Angeles Times*, December 5, 1977, p. 1.
2. Reported on the NBC television program, "Weekend," January 7, 1978.
3. David and Beatrice Alexander, eds., *Eerdmans' Handbook of the Bible* (Grand Rapids: Wm. B. Eerdmans Publishing Co., 1973), p. 484.
4. See also Everett F. Harrison, ed., *Baker's Dictionary of Theology* (Grand Rapids: Baker Book House, 1960), pp. 461,462.
5. Merrill F. Unger, *Unger's Bible Dictionary* (Chicago: Moody Press, 1957), p. 927.
6. D. Martyn Lloyd-Jones, *Studies in the Sermon on the Mount* (Grand Rapids: Eerdmans Publishing Co., 1959), v. 2, p. 143.
7. Lloyd-Jones, *Studies in the Sermon on the Mount*, p. 145.
8. Among the many Proverbs that could apply are: being popular—15:1; 17:7; being a good student—4:7; 13:20; being successful—3:5,6; 16:3.

158

9. See especially Jesus' words in John 15:10-14; Luke 6:30-38; Mark 12:28-31. Also see Ephesians 4:32; Philippians 1:9-11; Colossians 3:12-17; Romans 12:9,10 for just a few key examples of one of the major themes in the New Testament.

Chapter 3
1. Adapted from *Decisions and Outcomes*, H.B. Gelatt, Barbara Varenhorst, Richard Carey, Gordon P. Miller (New York: College Entrance Examination Board, 1973), p. 6,7.

Chapter 4
1. Charles F. Pfeiffer and Everett F. Harrison, eds., *The Wycliffe Bible Commentary* (Chicago: Moody Press, 1962), p. 1104.
2. William Barclay, *The Gospel of John*, The Daily Study Bible (Edinburgh: The Saint Andrew Press, 1965), v. 2, p. 183.
3. See especially chapter 2, Alexander I. Solzhenitsyn, *The Gulag Archipelago* (New York: Harper and Row, Publishers, 1973).
4. "Would You Kill Idi Amin?" *Campus Life*, December, 1977, p. 57.
5. For other references on Jesus' deity see John 10:30; John 12:45; John 1:1; Matthew 3:17; Matthew 8:18.
6. Brother Lawrence, *The Practice of the Presence of God* (Old Tappan, NJ: Fleming H. Revell Co., 1895), p. 8.
7. Lawrence, *The Practice of the Presence of God*, p. 10.
8. Lawrence, p. 32.
9. Lawrence, p. 34.
10. Lawrence, p. 35.
11. Lawrence, p. 44.

Chapter 5
1. Ralph Keyes, *Is There Life After High School?* (Boston: Little, Brown & Co., 1976,), pp. 16-18.
2. Robert H. Schuller, *Self Love: The Dynamic Force of Success* (Old Tappan, NJ: Spire Books, 1975), pp. 15-22.
3. John Piper, "Is Self-Love Biblical?," *Christianity Today*, August 12, 1977, pp. 6-9.
4. William Barclay, *The Gospel of Matthew*, The Daily Study Bible (Edinburgh: The Saint Andrew Press, 1956), v. 1, p. 401.
5. Charles M. Schulz, "Peanuts," United Features Syndicate, Inc., February 24, 1978.
6. George Sanchez, "The Scriptural Context for Realistic Self-Esteem," *Navlog*, January, 1978, p. 12.
7. Ken Olson, *The Art of Hanging Loose in an Uptight World* (New York: Fawcett Crest Books, 1974), p. 25.
8. Olson, *The Art of Hanging Loose*, ch. 5.
9. William Barclay, *The Letters to Philippians, Colossians and Thessalonians*, The Daily Study Bible (Edinburgh: The Saint Andrew Press, 1959), p. 99.
10. Barclay, *Philippians, Colossians and Thessalonians*, p. 99.
11. Other secular books dealing with self-esteem, to which you can apply

biblical principles include: Mildred Newman and Bernard Berkowitz with Jean Owen, *How to Be Your Own Best Friend* (Chicago: Valentine Books, 1974). Jess Lair, *I Ain't Much, Baby—But I'm All I've Got* (New York: Fawcett Crest Books, 1972). A good book on self-esteem written from a Christian perspective includes: James Dobson, *Hide or Seek* (Old Tappan, NJ: Fleming H. Revell Co., 1974).

Chapter 6
1. Earl G. Lee, *Recycled for Living*, (Glendale, CA: Regal Books, 1974), p. 4.
2. Lee, *Recycled for Living*, p. 6.
3. Lee, *Recycled for Living*, pp. 9,10.
4. Lee, *Recycled for Living*, p. 36.
5. Lee, *Recycled for Living*, p. 40, by Toki Miyashina, originally published in *Guideposts*.

Chapter 7
1. William Barclay, *The Gospel According to Matthew*, The Daily Study Bible (Edinburgh: The Saint Andrew Press, 1957), v. 2, p. 126.
2. Barclay, *Matthew*, v. 2, pp. 127-129.

Chapter 8
1. William Barclay, *The Gospel According to Matthew*, The Daily Study Bible (Edinburgh: The Saint Andrew Press, 1957), v. 2, pp. 227,228.
2. Adapted from Dwight H. Small, *Marriage: Handle with Care* (Glendale, CA: Regal Books, 1977), p. 3.
3. Adapted from H. Norman Wright, *Communication: Key to Your Marriage* (Glendale, CA: Regal Books, 1974), p. 52.
4. Wright, *Communication*, pp. 163-166.
5. "The American Family: Can It Survive Today's Shocks?" *U.S. News and World Report*, October 27, 1975, p. 32.
6. *Los Angeles Times*, March 30, 1978.

Chapter 9
1. D. Martyn Lloyd-Jones, *Studies in the Sermon on the Mount* (Grand Rapids: William B. Eerdmans Publishing Co., n.d.), p. 58.
2. William Barclay, *The Gospel According to Matthew*, The Daily Study Bible (Edinburgh: The Saint Andrew Press, 1959), v. 2, p. 92.
3. Barclay, *Matthew*, p. 92.
4. Lloyd-Jones, *Studies in the Sermon on the Mount*, p. 104.
5. Lloyd-Jones, *Studies in the Sermon on the Mount*, pp. 109,110.
6. Adapted from Edward R. Dayton and Ted W. Engstrom, *Strategy for Living* (Glendale, CA: Regal Books, 1976), p. 49.